The Side Hustle Bible

150+ Side Hustle Ideas and How to Start Making Money Right Away – Make Money Online and Offline

By Jacob Wallace

© **Copyright 2019 - All rights reserved.**

The content contained within this book may not be reproduced, duplicated or transmitted without direct written permission from the author or the publisher.

Under no circumstances will any blame or legal responsibility be held against the publisher, or author, for any damages, reparation, or monetary loss due to the information contained within this book. Either directly or indirectly.

Legal Notice:

This book is copyright protected. This book is only for personal use. You cannot amend, distribute, sell, use, quote or paraphrase any part, or the content within this book, without the consent of the author or publisher.

Disclaimer Notice:

Please note the information contained within this document is for educational and entertainment purposes only. All effort has been executed to present accurate, up to date, and reliable, complete information. No warranties of any kind are declared or implied. Readers acknowledge that the author is not engaging in the rendering of legal, financial, medical or professional advice. The content within this book has been derived from various sources. Please consult a licensed professional before attempting any techniques outlined in this book.

By reading this document, the reader agrees that under no circumstances is the author responsible for any losses, direct or indirect, which are incurred as a result of the use of information contained within this document, including, but not limited to, — errors, omissions, or inaccuracies.

Table of Contents

Introduction 7

Chapter 1: What Is a Side Hustle? 9

    What Is a Side Hustle? 9

    Side Hustles Vs. Second Jobs 10

    How Does a Side Hustle Work? 10

    How Can a Side Hustle Make You Rich? 11

    Why Is a Side Hustle Important? 12

    Things You Should Understand Before You Begin a Side Hustle 17

Chapter 2: Rules for Being Successful in Your Side Hustle 21

    How to Be Successful at Your Side Hustle When You Have a Full-Time Job 26

Chapter 3: Choosing Your Side Hustles 35

    Choosing the Appropriate Side Hustle Idea 35

    Questions to Ask Before You Choose a Side Hustle 42

    Is It Time to Turn Your Side Hustle into a Full-Time Business? 44

Chapter 4: Top Online Side Hustle Ideas 49

Chapter 5: More Side Hustle Ideas 74

Chapter 6: Side Hustles for Auto Mechanics 115

   Ways for Auto Mechanics to Make Extra Money 115

Chapter 7: Side Hustle for Programmers 118

Chapter 8: Side Hustle for Engineers 126

   What Can Engineers Do? 126

Chapter 9: Side Hustles for Graphic Designers 129

Chapter 10: Side Hustles for Teachers 139

Chapter 11: Side Hustles for Drivers 146

   Other Driving Jobs 150

   Be Your Own Boss 150

Chapter 12: Side Jobs for Law Enforcement Officers 152

Chapter 13: Side Hustles for Lawyers 155

Chapter 14: Side Hustles for Skilled Photographers 160

Chapter 15: Side Hustles for Models 168

Chapter 16: Best Side Hustles for Speakers 173

Chapter 17: Side Hustles for Musicians 176

Chapter 18: Side Hustle for Gamers 181

Chapter 19: Side Hustle for Animal Lovers 186

Chapter 20: Side Hustles for Accountants 191

Chapter 21: Side Hustles you can start for $10,000 to $50,000 194

Chapter 22: Side Hustles to Begin Under $10,000 199

Chapter 23: Conclusion 206

Introduction

With the hard and changing economic times, it is not realistic to survive on just one source of income alone. Yes, it is possible, but it is smarter to have more than one source of profits. This is where side hustles come in. However, there is a range of ideas for these side jobs existing today which can make it a bit tasking to make a choice.

Many individuals have tried and crashed even before the business picked up while others have done it and succeeded. So, why did some people succeed while others failed? The purpose of this book is to answer that question.

In the chapters to come, you will be learning all about side hustles. You will learn what it is and how to choose one. You will also learn which ones are ideal as part-time and those that are better as full-time. You will also be getting a basic idea of what you can expect to earn in any particular side hustle.

Lots of individuals are already taking advantage of this idea and are raking a decent amount of cash along with their regular income. So, how is this working out? Why are you not a part of this? If you feel you are not earning enough and would like to earn more income on the side, then this could be a helpful book for you.

There is no guarantee that you won't have to deal with hassles along the way. Starting anything new can be tasking. Nonetheless, I can assure you that when you are through with this book, which will be exposing you to more than 50 viable side hustles, you will have a clear idea on the kind you want to go into and all it entails.

Also, if you utilize all the information this book offers, you will thank yourself in a few years when you are making a decent amount of cash by the side or if you get to a position where you can end your job entirely and earn more than your salary from your side hustle. All of these resources aim to lead you to riches.

Chapter 1: What Is a Side Hustle?

Lots of individuals love boasting about their side hustles. But if you don't have one yet, and you need more cash but are not certain where to begin —maybe that's because you have no idea what a side hustle means and you may be feeling a bit confused.

Starting a side hustle is not difficult if you know what to do and where to begin. But before we go any further, let's look at what exactly it is.

What Is a Side Hustle?

A side hustle is any employment an individual takes on aside from his or her full job. Generally, a side hustle is freelance and offers extra income. These are usually things a person has a passion for, as opposed to a typical job they do just to make ends meet.

These side jobs are different from a part-time job. A part-time job has you reporting to another person, perhaps your employer, who calls the majority of the shots which include hours worked and the payment you will get. A side hustle offers you the freedom to determine the amount of what you want to do and cash you want to earn.

For most individuals, financial security is an issue, and side hustle proves to be a great choice for lots of individuals who are trying to be debt free or trying out entrepreneurship.

Side Hustles Vs. Second Jobs

At the thought of a side hustle, what comes to the minds of a lot of people is another job. Even though it has some things in common with a second job, they are very different.

The significant difference between a job and a side hustle is the fact that a side hustle is voluntary. As far as a job is concerned, you have to work for a certain period for a certain amount and carry out a particular task while a side hustle has a lot to do with entrepreneurship. In a side hustle, it is up to you decide on the kind of enterprise that you want to venture into. You also have the freedom to determine how long you intend to work every day, as well as how much money you want to make.

More often than not, people that are involved with side hustles make use of skills that they were able to acquire from their everyday jobs. Other times, they do things that they are passionate about, as well as things that they would do even if they were not being paid. A lot of people that own stores on Etsy are known to manage their stores as a form of side hustle. They do this with the aim of making some money from the skills that they have. This does not in any way imply that every form of side hustle needs a huge volume of experience or work. It also does not mean that they have to be associated with what one does full-time. Regardless of this, as a student, if you can learn more skills, the better your chances are of making a lot of money from a side hustle.

How Does a Side Hustle Work?

A side hustle is a job completed outside the daily job of an individual, and this sort of work tends to occur on the weekends, evenings, or during vacation breaks. It offers extra income while providing the flexibility to focus on your job.

You can begin your side hustle, or you can complete work on a contract, freelance, part-time, or on-call basis for an organization.

For individuals who are not ready to take that leap and quit their job or are scared of the vision of going into entrepreneurship, side hustles can offer an avenue to test ideas, explore passions, and develop a strong customer base if they do decide to give notice.

How Can a Side Hustle Make You Rich?

Earning some extra cash on the side is one thing. Even if the additional cash transforms into six figures, you are most likely not rich. So, how does a side hustle not only generate additional income, but also make you wealthy?

Take a look at the ways below:

Passive

This implies that your possible earning is not restricted by your time. You put in money or effort in advance and then start to earn cash indefinitely. You can achieve this via hiring individuals, investing, or owning intellectual property. Even side hustles like consulting can become larger and generate cash without you being involved as long as you can develop the appropriate team to do the job.

Scalable

Similar to passive income, scalable earning is not restricted by your time. But, it possesses another quality, which is the capacity to hit huge quantities. If you can sell 50 items or 2,000 items monthly without changing your direct effort too much, it means you have a scalable idea.

Sellable

Selling a business is an amazing method of earning a cash windfall. Say you sell your customer list, intellectual property, or an asset which produces income. You will observe that a few of the business ideas are not scalable, passive, or sellable.

This does not imply that it is not a good idea; it may be ideal for you and your situation. But as you expand and change, make efforts to utilize ideas that have the best possibility to give you financial freedom.

Why Is a Side Hustle Important?

Having a side hustle comes with a host of benefits which are both financial and otherwise. Below are a few of them:

Complete Accountability and Ownership

As the owner of a business, no one tells you what to do, and you can't blame anyone but yourself. This can be uncomfortable and scary when you initially begin your side hustle since you don't know how to work without someone telling you what to do. This ranges from your parents to your teachers to your team leads and managers.

If you can get past that, it is hugely empowering and motivating. It will enhance your confidence in your capacity, and also develop your resilience as you most likely will fail, which is normal when trying something new. However, you would be strong enough to get back up and keep going.

A Steeper Curve of Learning

Beginning your side hustle instantly places you in a sharp learning curve as you try navigating the complicated world of entrepreneurship. This provides you with all forms of experiences and skills that will test you and ensure that you are strong and capable.

There is a tremendous amount of development and growth that comes with heading out of the comfort zone of the job description you are probably working on and which you have probably been doing for a while.

Development and Self-Awareness

Discovering and working on your ideas can educate you on different things about yourself and things you like and don't like. Apart from the problem-solving skills you continue to learn as you operate your business, you will also be investing in your personal development.

In the corporate world, it is easy to depend on the training programs your employer offers. However, with you as the owner of the business, your development will be much faster, and you will be more well-versed in your skills and understanding of your weaknesses and areas you excel in.

A Sense of Direction

A familiar feeling many individuals have after being in a role for too long is that they lose their sense of direction and what their work means. Having a side hustle will aid in rejuvenating you with a new sense of direction and energy as you emphasize on something you have a passion for.

When running a business of your own, you will be directly interacting with customers and clients, and you will have a tangible and abrupt impact on all the things you lay your hands on in the business.

New Opportunities and Contacts

Just researching and talking to individuals about your idea will link you up with new connections and offer you opportunities that you could never have foreseen. The entire experience will also give you a competitive edge as your creativity and resourcefulness in beginning your side hustle helps you stand out from the crowd.

Whatever occurs with the organization itself, it is certain to put you on a path to success in your career.

Peace of Mind

The security of your regular job provides you the freedom to learn and try out new things without the pressure to make a considerable amount of cash instantly. Even if you have reasonable savings that make you comfortable enough to turn in your resignation, you might still begin to feel the fear coming in and that can be very draining and can sidetrack you from making your business successful.

Authenticating your business idea along with the comfort of your present job is a far more convenient method of getting things done.

Confidence

Beginning a side hustle while you are still in your regular job aids in assuring you of your value, thanks to the respect and responsibility work provides you, while your consistent salary means you would not be depending on the cash you are getting through your new side hustle.

This offers you the assurance to charge premium prices and

the capacity to leave a project if required. This is much better than when you have nothing else going on because you would feel forced to accept anything anyone pushes your way.

Work-Life Balance

While it may seem like including extra work to your plate will result in extra stress and minimize your free time further, that is not the case. It can aid you in achieving a work-life balance.

Now that there is something for you to do after work that you are excited and passionate about, you will be able to set better boundaries and ensure that you are not allowing your office job to spill into the weekends and evenings.

Outlet for Creativity

A side hustle gives you the opportunity to be more creative than your standard full-time job. If you have seen a child play with LEGOs, you will notice how creative they are. However, society wrecks the majority of this creativity as they grow. It gets replaced with the urge to earn cash and the requirement to have a standard job.

However, a side hustle can aid in re-awakening your creative side. So, if you enjoy developing furniture, DIY projects in your home, or creating music, a side hustle can aid you in selling your custom-made furniture, DIY projects, or music lessons.

When you can turn something you have a passion for into a side hustle, it gives you the opportunity to have an outlet for creativity while earning some cash on the side.

Additional Income

If you are stressed out consistently about living from paycheck to paycheck, having extra sources of income is one of the primary reasons for getting a side hustle.

Earning additional income will aid you in saving up for a down-payment on a home, paying off your student loan, saving for an emergency trip, or paying for a vacation. Regardless of your reasons, earning additional income on the side is a great thing.

By having a side hustle, you will have the capacity to achieve your financial objectives faster. More importantly, it can transport you to success moving forward.

You Have Something to Fall Back on

There is a common saying that goes, "Never place all your eggs in a single basket." So, why then would you depend on one source of income to support your financial objectives and pay your bills?

By getting a side hustle, you are making sure you have something to fall back on in the event that something unforeseen occurs. It is your plan B and safety net if your primary source of income does not work out.

Learn New Things

Irrespective of the side hustle you decide to go with, you will enhance your skills and grow as a person. A side hustle is a continuous work in progress, and it will only be a success if you desire to keep learning.

If you want to begin your side hustle business, nothing beats venturing into entrepreneurship to help you learn numerous things — these range from learning about networking, to developing a website, to learning SEO. You will be adding to your arsenal of knowledge from every angle.

Things You Should Understand Before You Begin a Side Hustle

Before starting a side hustle, there are a few things you should learn. Below are a few of them.

Carefully Think About Why You Want to Start a Side Hustle

Regardless of the type of side hustle you decide to go with, side-hustling is not an easy task. It is crucial to consider all your reasons for starting one by focusing on the way you would most enjoy making money in your free time.

If your primary motivation is because you are short on cash, maybe you could try a full-time career option with better pay. If you are genuinely passionate about your idea of starting a side hustle, would you be able to reduce the hours at your core place of work to make this possible?

Determining what role your side hustle has to play in your future career plan is crucial. Is it just a means of earning some more additional income while doing something you love, an economic requirement you hope to let go of the instant you have more financial security, or a dream that you would desire to be able to pursue completely once it kicks off?

Clearly defining your reasons for taking up an extra role is essential to determine how much energy and time you are ready to invest.

Understand That Finding Work Could Be Half the Journey

Most individuals are usually not ready for reality when they begin a side hustle. Side hustles have to do with you completing the job you need to do. This is because, as a matter of necessity, most second jobs occur outside of your normal office hours. There is a higher likelihood that side-hustlers will take up freelance jobs or depend on the gig economy. This implies that a lot of them need to search for new opportunities continuously.

The enormous task of having to look for your side hustle can feel demoralizing and testing. You need to be ready for rejections and numerous hours invested without any benefits. But the great news is that when the offers begin to come it, it is all worth it in the end.

Expect a Sluggish Start and Lots of Hard Work

If you have decided that your side hustle does not consist of flexible work or freelancing, then you need to expect the kick-off to be sluggish. Garnering interest in your work and developing a client base or contacts requires time, and the cash may not begin to come in from the start. After all, if it were not difficult, then it would most likely be your core source of income, right?

Be ready to invest lots of time without immediate benefits as regards cash. Accept that you may have to be flexible with your work or prices at the start with less popular clients. You need to be open-minded when it has to do with the work you are ready to take on.

Be Ready to Make Sacrifices

If you have plans to invest extra time in your side hustle, you need to let go of something else. Perhaps it is your gym time or the time you spend drinking with friends during the week or the time you spend seeing movies in the evening.

It can be difficult to let go of those things that are crucial to you, but if you plan on making your side hustle a success, then those declined invites will seem minor in comparison to the triumph of being successful in your work.

Create Boundaries

Although side hustles can offer lots of benefits, there is also a range of drawbacks. Working for more than 40 hours weekly has been associated with a host of physical and mental issues. These could range from depression, cardiovascular disorders, and anxiety. Unfortunately, the stress from working a full-time job and running a side hustle can be very demanding.

Making sacrifices could be crucial to running a fruitful side hustle, but you need to set boundaries to prevent burnout. Exercise, interpersonal relationships, and downtime are vital to your mental and physical well-being. So, if you observe that you are battling to balance these areas of your life with the needs of your second job, you need to stop and analyze how you can manage your time better.

Having specific evenings in place that are always work-free periods and making sure that you still have social events on your calendar can aid in keeping a balance between your personal and professional life.

Remain Organized

Doing a side hustle requires a lot of admin that is likely already done for you in a standard workplace. Doing invoices, accounts, and going through self-employment taxes are only a few of the troubles you may face in the long run if you plan on taking up a side hustle.

Although there is no method of getting around the additional extra work that has to do with side-hustling, being organized can be of great help. Make sure that you have a copy of all your paperwork saved, find out the deductions or subsidies you may be qualified for if you are a gig worker, and be ready to do your taxes beforehand. If your side hustle is providing you large business, it may be ideal to set a day of the week aside to do admin or get the services of an accountant to do it on your behalf once in a while.

Plan When and if You Want to Quit

If you find that your side hustle is bringing in a lot of cash, you may have to deal with a tough decision. Do you have plans to turn it into a full-time gig and if yes, when is the right time to leap?

For lots of individuals, a side hustle is just what it is: an extra job taken only for the fun of it and earning some additional funds. For others, a side hustle is an aspirational role or a dream that they would love to be able to invest themselves in entirely if they can be certain it would provide them support.

It can be scary to decide to switch careers. As a matter of fact, for lots of individuals, it may not feel like the appropriate time to let go of a stable job and commit to a venture that poses more risk. For this reason, it is essential that you have a clear plan from the start where you want your side hustle to direct you.

How much do you have to earn from your side hustle to be able to support yourself? Is there a timeline for when you would like your side hustle to ideally have risen to a full-time job? Being realistic and clear about your financial requirements can aid in giving you the push you may need to change your side hustle into your primary source of income.

Chapter 2: Rules for Being Successful in Your Side Hustle

The process of beginning a side hustle is not complicated. In just a few hours, your small business can be up and running. However, making a side hustle bring in cash, both personally and professionally is much more difficult.

The great news is that there are a few rules that can assist you with this. Some of these rules have worked for scores of individuals and should certainly help you in achieving your side hustle goals as well.

Below are some of these major rules.

Do Not Ignore Your Full-Time Job

Side hustles are fun. However, they can be a distraction, and it is enticing to dwell on, think about, and even work on your side hustle occasionally when you are supposed to be concentrating on your full-time job.

This is not a good idea. First, it is not the right thing to do. Second, you are likely not that subtle. Irrespective of how you go about it, someone is bound to notice. No matter what dreams you may have for your side hustle, if it is not cashing in enough to support you completely, you can't afford to lose your full-time income.

When you begin a side hustle, your objective is to be amazing at two things: your side hustle and your full-time job.

So, before you begin your side hustle in the first place, you need to focus on excelling at your full-time job. Work as efficiently and hard as you can. Do more than any other person. Do this so you can leave at the right time without regrets and without developing any concerns as regards your dedication and performance.

Don't Go into Debt for Your Side Hustle

Lots of businesses need funds for overhead and running costs before they can make cash. It is for this reason that lots of companies take a long time before bringing in profit. A large portion of startups run down because of their inability to bring in profit.

How would you be able to avert this? Begin a side hustle that you can finance via your savings, or better still, one that does not require funding. Offer a service that only needs the tools you already have. Sell products that you will be able to either produce or purchase by consignment. Establish the fact that a market is available, and you will have the capacity to serve that market before taking on any debt.

Buying things you believe would make your business profitable may be tempting but its best to hold off on. The only actual business is that that provides you a profit which is more difficult when you are repaying debt that you could have avoided in the first place.

If you are unable to find a method to begin your side hustle without taking debt, you need to search for another idea.

Your Side Hustle Should Not Be an Excuse

Imagine you start a side hustle that has to do with using your vehicle for pick-ups. You have always wanted to get a new car, so you started a side hustle, then you purchased the new vehicle.

But presently, you don't need it; you only want it.

Lots of side-hustlers who have failed admit that they began their business as a method of rationalizing the purchase of something they always desired. It could be a better car because "I want my clients to have a great impression of me" or new clothes "because my hustle needs me to look great."

If you desire something, there is nothing wrong about it, but don't start a side hustle as a reason to purchase it.

Don't Spend Cash That Your Clients Won't See.

You may have a fantastic office at your full-time job. You may have great amenities, but don't believe your side hustle should also.

Before spending any cash, always ask yourself, "Does this have a direct impact on my client?" If it does not, then don't purchase it.

Spend the cash you have where it makes a significant difference to your clients. This is because when there are no clients, you have no side hustle.

Only Spend Cash When It Is Essential

It may seem like a great idea to think ahead, to predict needs, and then spend some money using those predictions like requiring more supplies before there is a demand, requiring more tools before a demand comes in, or requiring higher efficiency before you have to be that efficient. Yes, purchasing a specific tool can aid you in performing particular tasks quicker, but if presently, you don't have adequate clients that will pay you to carry out that task, don't purchase it.

Let yourself be inefficient until there is adequate work to ensure that more efficiency is crucial.

Go with a Strict Schedule for Your Side Hustle

When your typical workday is over, work on your side hustle is just starting. Determine the number of hours you believe you can spend daily on your side hustle. Now, add 30-50 percent to that number. If you are considering one hour, let it be two or three instead.

Then, follow this schedule. Write it down, and if your schedule states that you need to work from 5 p.m. to 8.p.m. each evening, and from 8.a.m. to 5.p.m. every weekend, ensure you work during those periods.

Look at the schedule you develop for your startup just the way you would see that of your present job; treat it as extremely important. Then, work with that schedule; otherwise, you will be unable to see any development. You will also be discouraged quickly, and will never provide yourself a chance to be successful.

Have Huge Dreams but Narrow Your Focus

Almost every side-hustler has a vision of finding a great client that will aid you in going past the hustle and actually kick-starting a business.

But in reality, not many people find that ideal client. As opposed to finding a means of making millions in cash, look for ways of serving millions of customers. Begin small, and have a vision of where you would have a great chance of success.

As time goes on, you will develop your skills. You will also develop a customer base. Later on, you will be able to leverage this customer base successfully.

Only Do Things That Bring in Cash

Yes, you may have to spend some time on infrastructure and admin, but not too much. You don't require elaborate reports or a fancy spreadsheet. You equally don't require an appealing mission statement or brand.

So, what do you require? You need work. One that will ensure you get paid. Side-hustlers emphasize two core things which are working and selling.

It may be true that when you do the things you love, money will come, but this is the case only if you are doing what brings in revenue. If it fails to pay, put it aside.

Entrepreneurs who are successful spend extra time working on their business instead of in their business. This may be the case for you as well later in future, but presently, a successful side hustle needs you to work in the business, and this is because it is the only period you earn cash.

Always Take Action

It is great to make plans, but anything could happen. Lots of individuals who begin a side hustle don't survive past their initial three action items before they are faced with reality. Spend some time planning, and spend more time taking action. If you are not certain, do something, and then respond appropriately.

It is not difficult to think, plan, and analyze yourself out of ever beginning a side hustle in the first place. Do not forget that it is not a life and death affair, and it is just a side hustle. See the beginning of a side hustle as the experiment that it is. Always remember that the fun is not in thinking but in doing.

View Your Side Hustle as Your Time

When you pick a side hustle, go with something you want to achieve and want to do. Choose something you desire to be, and work toward it actively.

Aside from the fact that you would benefit from the sense of triumph that you get from heading toward a goal, even if the objective is doing something solely for fun, it will make you feel better about your life and yourself.

You should see your side hustle time as personal time. This is because it is time you spend making the best out of your life. See it as a time that will leave you with a high feeling of fulfillment.

Yes, your friends may be having fun in other ways, which could be their time. The same can also be said about a side hustle because when you select the appropriate side hustle, and you invest your all, it implies that you are making the best of every moment you have.

This perfectly defines personal time and is the best method of actually living.

How to Be Successful at Your Side Hustle When You Have a Full-Time Job

The best method of eventually becoming your boss is to begin a side hustle and grow your self-employed revenue, while you still have the security and safety of your full-time job.

The great news is that beginning a side hustle is not only padding your income, but it also provides you with career-changing chances that you would not have come across normally during your full-time job. Numerous side hustles have become new jobs, beneficial relationships, and lifetime acquaintances.

But, developing a side hustle to bring in cash with the prescribed amount of time outside your full-job is not so straightforward. It requires serious prioritizing, a shift on the way you view things that are most crucial in your life, and the willingness to get scrappy and creative daily.

If you want to take the path of entrepreneurship, there are a handful of reasons you need to begin small with growing your side hustle from one customer to another from nothing. The possibility of earning cash apart from your normal paying job is a major incentive, especially in this unstable economy. A hobby you have been nurturing for a long time can also inspire you to grow a business around those things you desire.

Would-be entrepreneurs with a powerful drive can use a side hustle as a means toward attaining financial freedom. Your side hustle can give you the opportunity to emphasize what matters most to you, especially if your full-time job does not offer you a similar satisfaction. It can offer you the flexibility and additional savings to care for the environment, travel the globe, or chase causes in a more significant manner.

A huge number of individuals have kicked-off a side hustle that has to do with consulting, freelancing, and a host of other businesses based online while doing a regular job. Speaking factually, as stated in a study by LinkedIn ProFinder in 2016, over 300,000 experts in just the United States are doing freelancing along with their regular jobs.

While lots of individuals will inform you that they have dreams and hopes of going into entrepreneurship, the other side of the picture is not as fascinating. Most of the new businesses out there are not set up for success.

Part of attaining success as an entrepreneur means that you have to begin small and build with your clients. This is where side hustle can be of help. If you have plans to begin a side hustle, the steps below will aid in keeping you ahead while you keep your full-time job as your source of constant income.

Be Ready for the Long Haul

If you have a great service or product, you won't get anywhere if you don't have the determination, grit, and actual interest in aiding your future clients to provide solutions for actual issues. So, before beginning a side hustle, you need to ask yourself how bad your desire for success is. If you are playing with a business idea and entertaining the concept of making it big, don't think you will become successful in one night or you will become discouraged right away.

Don't forget that your side hustle will start to take numerous hours weekly from those moments you would usually be spending with family, friends, and other locations. A side hustle also needs a lot of effort on your part to be successful given that most of your time daily would be channeled to your full-time job.

Make an analysis on whether or not this is something you are willing to do. If you are ready to make this sacrifice, create a system of positive routines and triggers to aid in supporting your self-discipline, and apply all your additional effort in growing your side hustle, then you would have the psychological footing to establish a successful side hustle.

Point Out Your Areas of Interest and Skill

Never go into a fight without the proper equipment for the issues that will come your way. If you want to experience rapid results, you have to support your side hustle with the appropriate experience, skills, or knowledge of the industry. After all, success in business is only possible when the appropriate skills meet the proper areas of interest. Your business is only likely to succeed if it is something you love doing, and you are great at it.

For example, lots of musicians earn cash from their skill by providing lessons to others. Some creative experts also have well-paying freelance side hustles as digital story writers or graphic designers. If you do not have the core skills that have to do with your interests or the side hustle you want to develop, now is the best time to learn them.

Endorse Your Side Hustle with One Paying Client

To you, your side hustle idea may seem very disruptive and awesome, but your potential customers may not see it that way. Oftentimes, they will ignore a huge portion of amazing ideas because of the huge amounts of daily advertisements and distractions we come across daily.

The actual reason you need validation for your side hustle with a paying client before you head too far in the business is to ensure you are not developing a solution to an issue that is not in existence.

So, you need to be aware that there is a huge possibility that you are growing an idea that not enough individuals will see as valuable. And if there isn't anyone who wants your service or product, all of the resources you invested in its development will be a waste.

To ensure this does not occur, be certain to validate if your service or product will gain a pull in the actual world. You will be able to do this by getting objective feedback from possible clients and request that they become a part of a waiting list, pay for your services as a service provider, or pre-purchase your product. Quickly let go of ideas that are not providing you with the response you desire and consider more realistic opportunities.

Make Yourself Stand Out from Competitors

If you have created a completely new service or product that is in a class of its own, there is a possibility that you would be placing your side hustle against other players that have already cornered a part of the market, catering to the same target clients. Competition is an aspect of doing business that you can't avoid. In almost any niche, competitors will try to do better than your service or product, take as many clients as they can, and look for chances to do better than you.

To avert this from occurring, all you have to do is utilize serious competitive advantage. Your competitive edge could be something that makes your business unique from that of your competitors. This could include aggressive sales tactics, strategic relationships, low or smart pricing, increased profit margins, intellectual property, and unmatched customer service alongside other specific factors that make your brand distinct from the competition.

Your competitive advantage is what makes clients select you and keep heading back for more.

Have Clear Goals

It is not a bad idea to have huge dreams. However, when it has to do with ensuring that your side hustle becomes a success, you won't get anywhere if you aim for the final position from the start. To ensure you achieve your larger goals, you have to begin with smaller goals. After you get one satisfied client, it's time to move on to your second, third, and so on.

If you start by aiming for 2,000 clients as opposed to one, you will get stunned with everything that has to be ready before dealing with lots of customers.

Having practical goals that you can attain weekly, daily, and monthly can aid you in developing positive habits and grooming yourself for success. One great framework to utilize when creating goals is the SMART goals Criteria. It stands for Specific, Measurable, Achievable, Relevant, and Time-bound.

Create Milestones That Will Push You to Launch

A viable and good side hustle idea has to be kicked-off, monetized, and repeated. Don't fixate yourself trying to develop the ideal solution when you are not certain of what your customers are drawn to the most. If you do this, you will end up wasting valuable time, stuck in a dream state without taking any action. To aid you in beating this, draw a simple plan for action that lays out crucial deadlines and milestones that will direct you from when you begin until launch date. Follow set deadlines, inform family and friends about them, hold yourself liable, and don't let yourself make excuses.

Then carry out the action that is required to head from one milestone to another. Remember, never target perfection because it will draw you back and keep you from launching anything.

Delegate Jobs Not in Your Expertise

By now, since you are aware of your strengths, you can always be great at everything, but you should not strive to be. The reality of beginning a side hustle is that you are going to possess weaknesses. This implies that a few or a lot of the skills required in running your side hustle efficiently must be located in another location so you can free up your time to keep doing just the things you are great at in your business.

For example, you may be a great graphic designer, but your admin skills will easily chase off your targets instead of keeping them engaged. To solve this, do just the things you are great at and work at delegating other parts. Delegating your weak points is an alternative which is easier to implement and more efficient.

In the long run, it is also more cost-effective as the value of your time goes up significantly.

Request for Actual Customer Feedback

Without getting feedback from your initial clients, you will leave your side hustle open to a severe possibility of failure. You may have plans to produce a service or product that does not do the best job possible in solving the problems of your clients. Without external, objective feedback, you will probably execute the plan, invest reasonable money, effort, and time in the process, only to lose all of these precious resources in the end.

By making it a routine to internalize strict feedback, you will push yourself to keep making improvements to your solutions as you go forward.

Ensure You Don't Lose Your Full-Time Job

It is not ideal that you work on your side hustle during the time you should be working for your full-time job. Also, you should not use the resources of the company to achieve your personal goal. Aside from being unethical, it is probably a violation of the agreements you signed when you started the job.

Make it compulsory to honor every aspect of your contract and to continuously provide amazing performances during your full-time job while your side hustle grows. Compromising your reputation and work quality in the office will avert you from re-engaging and even possibly collaborating with your past employers once you become a full-time entrepreneur.

The most important fact is that not complying with the terms of the contract can result in legal and even disciplinary action which would cost you even more cash that you could have invested in your side hustle.

Develop a Consistent Flow of Clients Before You Quit Your Day Job

It is best never to leave your full-time job till your side hustle is offering you an increasing and sustainable cash flow that gets to no less than 75 percent of what you earn from your full-time job. Lots of entrepreneurs are risk takers, but you should not head into anything without having a decent possibility of succeeding.

Also, it is best to have no less than 5 months of savings for both business and personal purposes to supplement yourself if your business does not develop a fast as you planned. Don't forget that having customers who are excited and transforming them into earnings in the early parts of your side hustle is the major sign of success in the future. If you have a family depending on you, stay away from the urge to resign immediately until you are prepared.

Being Successful with Your Side Hustle

According to data, new businesses have a low probability of

attaining success. However, this should not impede you from chasing a more meaningful self-employed job. The best period to grow a business is when you have income from a full-time job that aids in covering all your living costs. Consider your normal employment as protection against the risks you are taking as you try out how viable your side hustle is.

Chapter 3: Choosing Your Side Hustles

If you are in search of a way to begin a side hustle and begin to earn more cash on your way, you might be thinking of what kind of work you can do.

There are numerous types of side hustles available, so how can you determine the appropriate one for you?

Choosing the Appropriate Side Hustle Idea

Everyone is looking to choose the idea that has the most likelihood of succeeding. However, the idea itself is not important; more critical is choosing the appropriate client.

Any business can be successful if you try to serve the appropriate individuals, but this is not as easy to think about as opposed to just choosing an idea, so it does not get as much attention. This is bad because, in the long run, your micro-business is unable to survive by being unique, cutting edge, or entertaining. It survives because it is useful.

Selecting a customer segment is more difficult than choosing an idea because an idea is something you will be able to understand completely in your head and does not need any input from another person to feel great about it. If the idea seems nice to you, you are going to be glad. That is until you begin and observe that nobody likes the idea.

Instead, begin with a customer. This is more difficult because the initial thing you have to do is to point out the issue individuals are having, and understand the issue properly enough to proffer a solution. Also, the solution can't be one you believe is great. It has to equally be great to other people.

This does not have to be a complex or stressful process. Locating a great customer for your side hustle only needs a few steps. Take a look at them below:

Who Is the Client and What Is Their Issue?

The more precise you can be when providing an answer to this question, the more success you will likely have.

Don't be deceived by the theory that if your business helps in solving a common issue for everyone, it will be a success. There is a higher likelihood that it will be too basic, and everyone will end up ignoring it.

Instead, you need to focus. Think of issues that you have faced in your daily life that you provided solutions for by yourself. You can utilize yourself as a case study if you can locate others that have a similar issue.

- Bad example: My client is a man who requires better shoes.

- Good example: My client is a single man in his 20s who requires better office shoes.

- Better example: My client is a single business person in his 20s who requires better office shoes for his meetings with clients.

The more explicit you are, the better. This is because when you develop a precise image of your customer in your head, it makes answering the next two questions which are vital for the success of your side hustle easier.

Can My Client Afford to Pay?

Taking a look at the profile you created for your client, does this seem like the kind of person that has the resources to pay for what you are offering? The more detailed you get, the less difficult it would be for you to answer this question. If your answer is not yes, you need to begin from step one again.

Is My Client Ready to Pay?

This is the next qualifier which is no less crucial than the initial one. Your clients could have lots of cash and not have any idea what they want to use it for, but if they don't see the issue you believe they have and don't find it valuable, or they don't feel the pain it causes, then irrespective of how amazing your offer is, they won't pay for it.

Also, if the answer to this is still no, then you need to head back to step 1.

Create a List of Your Interests and Skills

Another great method of determining the side hustle that would be appropriate for you is to develop a list of all your interests and skills.

Side-hustling can be time consuming, especially if you consider the fact that you have other life responsibilities, including a regular full-time or part-time job. It is important to ensure you select a side hustle that you are great at and can enjoy. This way, it won't seem like an additional chore. Take some time to reflect and think when you put this list together and consider all your interests and skills.

Are you a great singer? Do you write well? Are you a fan of social media? Do you love speaking to other individuals? Do you do well in specific academic subjects?

Even if you love to do something as easy as playing with pets or organizing, place it down on your list because it will aid you in finding focus as you gather ideas for your side hustle.

Be Truthful About Your Availability

The instant you have your list of interests or skills, you may already have some amazing ideas for a profitable side hustle you can try out.

Before leaping ahead to this aspect, it is crucial to think about the amount of energy and capacity you will have to invest in a side hustle. Be truthful about your present schedule and how changes can occur. How many days do you normally get off at your actual job? Would you have any free time in the morning, weekends, or evenings to invest in your side hustle?

You most likely don't want to be working 24/7, but it is ideal to come up with a realistic timeframe you can put aside for your side hustle weekly. This could be 3 – 30 hours each week. It is all dependent on your availability and schedule.

Also, remember to consider your levels of energy. Look at the moment you have high amounts of energy during the day to invest in making more cash. For some individuals, this is during the morning or afternoon while some other individuals work better in the evenings.

If you know you won't have the energy or time to get out of work and engage in your side hustle, you may want to select some flexible work you will be able to do before heading to work.

Explore Potential for Income

Next, determine the amount of extra cash you want or have to earn. Side hustles are often pushed by our financial objectives, so it is sensible to comprehend what your financial requirements are before you become commit to anything.

Ask yourself the reason you want to begin a side hustle. You want to earn more cash, but why?

Maybe you have debts to pay off or need to replace your full-time income with a work from home opportunity. The instant you have clarified the reason why, select an income goal that suits your circumstances.

Not every side hustle is equal. Although some of them may require low-effort and be fun, they could have a potential for low-earning, so that is something to note.

If you only desire to earn additional cash, so you can head to more happy hours and brunches with your friends, you may see that side hustles like mystery shopping or taking surveys online can be a great fit.

If you would rather earn $200 every month to pay for one of your bills or support your home payment, you may observe that pet sitting, dog walking, or a part-time job at a retail store would be significant.

However, if you are looking to earn $400 and above monthly, you may want to take a look at some of the following side hustles which have more earning potential:

- Freelance Writing

- Pinterest Virtual Assistant

- Photography

- <u>Driving for Uber</u>
- Coaching/Consulting
- <u>Virtual Assistant</u>
- Graphic Design/ Programming
- <u>Airbnb</u>
- Private Tutoring
- Blogging

Determine When You Would Begin to Earn Additional Cash

When most individuals find out about side hustling or start to nurture the concept of beginning a side hustle, all they see is the cash they have the potential to make.

While the money side can be amazing, you need to understand that you may not begin making cash immediately.

There are side hustles like being an Uber or Lyft driver which would let you earn cash faster because there is a weekly payment. Other side hustles take more time to pay out, and if you are considering going into blogging or freelancing, you may not make much cash at all at the start.

The nice aspect about freelancing is that you can be flexible which means you can determine your rates alongside the number of hours you work. But, it might require some weeks to get new clients, especially if you do not have adequate experience. You may have to offer trial services for lower than your desired rate when you are beginning so you would get some experience.

With blogging, you may not be able to earn any cash in the initial months. But if you keep going on, it will keep paying off consistently. Some side hustles are ideal for short-term, quick incomes while others may need you to invest your cash and time, but will become a major income source you can rely on in the long run. It's left for you to determine what you are searching for presently.

Narrow Down Your Choices

Now, you need to narrow down your available choices since you are aware of what your skills and interests are, your income goals, your availability to work, and the amount of time you are willing to hold on to before you start to generate revenue.

It will be a great idea to put down your top choices. List out the pros and cons alongside other implications of each of them. Compare, contrast, and see the side hustle idea that seems like a great match.

This process will take more time that it would for others. You may have already decided a leading side hustle in one of the first steps, or you might spend more time evaluating your choices. There is no perfect way of doing this.

When you do make your choice, it should feel right and something that should excite you.

Questions to Ask Before You Choose a Side Hustle

By asking yourself these questions, you may have a rich picture of the type of hustle you are in search of or the kind of side hustle that is suitable for your circumstances.

Do You Require a Work-At-Home Job Only as a Side Hustle Without Any Additional Expertise?

If you are in search of a job you can do from home as a side hustle to meet your financial needs without having to bother about lots of qualifications, then you have numerous choices to select from.

Note that if you are searching for side hustles similar to these, you will not be earning as much as your full-time job offers but just some additional funds.

The following are options you can dabble into:

- Website testing
- Online English Tutor
- Flipping
- Evaluators of Search Engines
- Chat Agents
- Online Mystery Shopper

Are You in Search of a Part-Time Job You Can Do After Work Hours?

There are numerous jobs you can do from home that are part-time and flexible. You will certainly be able to tailor them around your schedule. Part-time work options are ideal if you are in search of something alongside your job or if you want to do something when your children are at school. There are numerous organizations to help you, such as Wonder and Appen Butler.

You will be able to locate job roles like virtual assistants, customer service, and freelance writers among a host of others.

Is This Income Going to Be a Replacement for Your Primary Income in the Long Run?

If you have a plan to replace your primary income with a job you can do from home, then you should have a diverse search method. You should be in search of jobs that you can do from home which are not sporadic or seasonal and can transform into a significant stream of income.

At times, it may be a lengthy process to transform your side hustle into a significant source of income, but the potentials are limitless. The side hustles you can do that can offer you this opportunity are:

- Bookkeeping
- Proofreading
- E-commerce Store
- Virtual Assistant

Do You Have Plans to Develop Your Hobby into a Business?

Nowadays, earning cash from your hobby is indeed a possibility, and growing it into a business which brings in revenue is quite common. You may dabble into lots of things like cooking, blogging, selling online, professional organizing, and crafts among a host of others. You would also be able to develop these into a business which makes you money. Do note that if you have plans to establish a business, you will need to invest a bit in inventory and websites among others.

If you have plans to learn new things via side hustling, then you have a lot of things to select from depending on what you plan on doing. Today, with lots of new streams of earning cash, there is a possibility that you can make some money from it. Ranging from graphic design to blogging, there are numerous avenues you can learn from and earn some money. Websites like Udemy and others can offer you amazing insights into a few of these new side hustles.

Do You Have Plans of Managing Your Full-Time Job Alongside Your Side Hustle?

It can be quite tasking to manage your side hustle alongside your main job. However, if you have put down a plan, it can be less complex from the beginning. Be specific about your target and the reasons you are beginning to do a side hustle so that you would have fixed expectations. This can affect your productivity significantly and make your job less complicated. Managing a side hustle along with your full-time job can be tasking, but it is not impossible.

Is It Time to Turn Your Side Hustle into a Full-Time Business?

Over 50 million individuals who make more than 30 percent of the workforce in the United States are now contractors or freelancers. By 2020, this number has been projected to go up to 43 percent.

A side hustle can aid in complementing your day job and can

offer useful security against the uncertainty of the economy and a method of developing new skills. This is because even as the cost of living continues to rise, salaries and wages don't tend to change. This is why side hustles are becoming increasingly popular.

In some situations, it starts to seem that your side hustle takes up the majority of your time as opposed to your core position, and in most cases, you are passionate about your side hustle. After a while, you may begin to ask yourself if your side hustle should be your full-time source of income.

For lots of individuals, determining when they should transform their side hustle into a major business is the most tedious part. If you are in this category, how do you know when you should make this crucial decision?

The following are signs that can help you decide.

You Are Earning More Than Enough

Although lots of us have the desire to support ourselves doing what we enjoy, in many situations, it is just not feasible. After all, irrespective of the level of passion you have for something, in the end, it must be able to support you.

To explain this clearly, a side hustle is only a hobby until you can attain some form of monetary gain from it, and the instant you begin to earn cash, it can be a while before you start earning any substantial income.

That being said, if your side hustle has kicked off, and you notice yourself getting about the same amount or higher than your normal job, then it may be time to do it full-time. In the end, you need to make sure that what you earn from your side hustle is adequate, close, or more than enough to sustain your lifestyle and expenses.

It Is Taking Up All Your Time

As your side hustle continues to grow, it will inevitably require more time. When this occurs, you will start to see yourself drawn into numerous directions.

As opposed to common belief, it is almost impossible to offer your all into numerous endeavors. This could result in your day job taking the back seat or becoming ignored. You most likely have a manager at your full-time job, and when you slack, it would certainly be noticed soon.

If you find yourself strained for time, it could be the right time to offer your full attention to your side hustle, before your trying to manage both pulls in unnecessary attention.

You Are Doing Well Being Your Boss

It is not easy to own your business. It involves more than just doing the task you have developed it around. Also, it is difficult to remain motivated and staying on-task when you have an external force such as your supervisor whose role is making certain you do your job.

However, if you have attained a sustainable and steady pace for yourself and can meet all the deadlines you have created for yourself, then you may be able to become your boss because the great aspect about transforming your side hustle into a full-time gig is that you ultimately become your own boss.

You Have Developed a Well-Laid Out Plan

Even the leading plans can fail, and this includes a business plan. Beginning and keeping business is tough and lots of individuals fail at it. You should not stop your full-time job for your side hustle impromptu. You need to plan better than that.

In essence, if you have invested time in creating a genuine business plan which shows future projections, and you have started to implement these plans, then you may have the appropriate tools to launch your business completely.

You Have a Consistent Business

Consistency is crucial for any business. No business will be able to exist on a few large commissions every year. In reality, they survive via consistent income that they can depend on. This is aside from the fact that there is less stress involved.

Passing the word out and getting projects or clients is the most challenging aspect when you are starting a side hustle. Until you have a steady foundation or base, it may not be realistic to go full-time. The instant you find yourself having a steady work or client flow with the ability or prospects to find new ones, you can then consider leaving your main gig for your side hustle.

You Are Passionate and Not Scared of the Unknown

It is safe to work 9-5 for a company owned by another individual. It is also quite predictable to a reasonable extent. Also, the success of the organization is not on you alone but a whole group of individuals.

If you want to transform your side business into your actual job, you need to be brave enough to head into the unknown just as numerous entrepreneurs before you. It should be a choice you make because you are passionate about the work you are doing. You need to have enough passion for putting in the hard work and time it will take in running a business by yourself.

It is going to be scary to make a career switch and go on by yourself. Even if you have a blooming side hustle, leaving a dependable full-time gig to chase your own business is full of challenges and risks that may seem scary.

However, if you have located a side hustle that you not only have a passion for but has risen into a job that can help in sustaining you, then without a doubt, you have accomplished the desire of lots of individuals. When it boils down to it, there are specific signs that your side hustle is more than just a side hustle. If you see that these signs are true, it may be the moment to reevaluate your full-time job.

Chapter 4: Top Online Side Hustle Ideas

There are loads of side hustle ideas available. Some are not that complex to start while others need small business capital and significant time to kick off. Below are some of the leading ideas which can help get started.

1. *Blogging*

Do you believe blogging is not a viable income source anymore? Well, this couldn't be more wrong. Numerous bloggers are developing profitable content on numerous topics ranging from travel, home cooking, business, lifestyle, personal finance, and many other topics.

More importantly, blogs can grow into businesses which would bring in vast amounts of profit thanks to a blend of blog sponsorships, affiliate marketing, email subscribers, and other streams of revenue. The first thing you need to learn when beginning a blog is to handle the technical aspect of things quickly. Then you need to have an understanding of what your audience desires, and learn how to draw in users online.

If you want to hasten the process of starting a blog, you can set up an affordable, easy, and quick website hosting with an organization like Bluehost, selecting an easy WordPress theme, and working on your initial post to set a practice of planning your time on connecting with your audience and creating content.

Then, when you are through building a community around your blog, you will want to invest in actually understanding those who read your content, so you can offer them more of what they desire.

2. Graphic Designing

Although having prior knowledge in graphic design is going to be beneficial, it is also not difficult to learn the basics of graphic design by yourself. There are tools which are easily accessible and easy to use like Adobe illustrator, Visme, and Stencil which make it very easy for anyone with a little creativity and two working thumbs to earn revenue from designing images.

You will also be able to add motivational quotes alongside your designs, transform them into posters, and sell them on platforms like Etsy. You can equally locate a small business owner, a local startup, or a photographer who could use the additional assistance in altering or designing images.

Before you begin to earn full-time as a graphic designer, you will have to develop your skills. Numerous online resources can be of help in this area.

3. Web Design

Web designers are very significant to technology companies. This is the reason why heading into freelance web designing is a leading business idea now. Web designing has to do with understanding the process of creating a value-driven and beautiful experience for individuals utilizing an application or website.

New websites that require professional design are always springing up which means there is good business for you in this field. To begin on the right path of deciding if web designing would be a great side business for you, there are online courses on platforms like Udemy which would teach you all you need to know about web designing to earning your initial income as a freelance web designer.

4. Web Development

As a web developer, you will develop treasured skills that are in high demand. You can learn about web development in just a little while with free and budget-friendly online education programs like Udemy, Treehouse, Codecademy, and Web Developer Bootcamp.

The instant you know Javascript, Ruby, HTML, CSS, or Python, you will be able to begin a side hustle in this while holding on to your full-time job and developing your portfolio.

As time goes on, you will have more experience, develop new relationships, and eventually make this side business your full-time gig.

5. Online Courses

Utilizing your skills to earn income is a popular trend with all the leading side hustle ideas. If you are proficient at something, there would possibly be a large number of individuals online who would gladly pay to become professionals in your field like you.

If you desire to take your skills and transform them into an online course which will teach others how to get results just like you have in your business, career, or life, there are lots of valuable courses you can take advantage of on Udemy.

The instant you are ready to begin your course online, you can utilize Teachable which is the most affordable and easiest platform to utilize for hosting, creation, and the sales of your online courses. They also provide a range of free educational resources about how you can begin developing an online course even as a business idea the instant you sign up.

6. *Writing eBooks*

Packaging your knowledge and skills into a downloadable eBook which offers value to individuals who want to go further in their careers, learn a skill, or begin their businesses, offer a powerful value proposition if you aim at the appropriate audience.

If you place significant work into developing your eBook and building your audience, you will have an avenue to pitch traditional publishers on getting you a book deal, then you can write one of the leading books in your field and develop your brand.

7. *Instagram Marketing*

If you can develop a decent amount of following on your Instagram account, lots of companies, brands, and other significant businesses that sell products and services that have to do with the kind of content you distribute on Instagram will quickly approach you. In turn, this would enable you to create numerous possible side hustle ideas that will come your way.

If you have the appropriate skills in marketing and a huge number of followers, you will be able to easily charge around $400 - $7,000 or above for every post which ensures it is a very viable side hustle idea. The instant you gain some popularity, to reduce the time you spend on uploading images, you can create a more efficient workflow by posting images from your PC or Mac.

8. Online Coaching

If you are skilled at something and very passionate about it, you can transform this winning combination into providing your services by coaching one-on-one online as a solid idea for a business. Just be certain to incorporate your opportunity management system, so you are not stuck working alongside clients that you cannot assist.

Aside from the experience and skill factors to being a prosperous online coach, this side hustle idea has to do with developing a community centered on the assistance you are providing and garnering trust with members. Also, the members of your community will learn from one another as time goes on. Developing a space for this form of a community can be easy as creating a private group on Facebook or selecting a platform for community building like Ning.com that even has more functionalities like having customized designs, using your custom URL, and having internal forums among a host of others.

9. Podcasting

If you can develop an audience for your podcast on a precise topic, it is an amazing way of attaining sponsors and sponsoring this side hustle idea. Naturally, it would be helpful if you already have an online audience you can take advantage of to listen to your recurring podcasts. Even if that's not the case, it has not prevented numerous amounts of individuals from developing podcasts into lucrative side hustles.

10. Reselling on Amazon

Any individual will be able to sell products on Amazon, as long as there are products to sell or purchase at a low price. If you are the kind of person to head to all the local garage sales every weekend, there are all kinds of valuable items you can resell online as a side hustle idea.

If you want to further your Amazon selling skills, take a look at this elaborate guide on Entrepreneur to [Amazon and eBay retail arbitrage](#) which features an interview with Julie Becker alongside many drop-shippers who have developed this business idea into a prosperous stream of income.

1. *Drop-Shipping*

This is an easy and amazing method of earning additional cash because you don't have to do any shipping and packing. However, you will have to create a website, so you can handle any frequent transactions.

How Does It Work?

You pick products to sell on platforms such as eBay and mark them. Say, for example, you list a computer keyboard on eBay for $20 that the drop shipper sells for $15. When you make a sale, you send the information of your buyer to the drop shipper alongside the $15 and you hold on to the remaining $5.

The drop shipper then sends the buyer the keyboard. You could have as much as 20 or 30 of those similar keyboards and end up making as high as $200 or more with very little effort. Now, it is very easy to list items on eBay and in less than an hour, you can list as much as 10 various items with ease.

Watchmen Advisors is a website that has a free list of confirmed drop-shipping suppliers. For example, it lists drop shippers in the categories of electronics, health and fitness, sporting goods, collectibles and gifts, and automotive among a host of others.

By completing a simple form, you will be provided with a complete list of these drop shippers. Select the ones that you have an interest in, and begin to list items.

The platform also offers internet marketing consulting and training and tips for small organizations. You could speak with someone in the organization to aid you with drop-shipping projects.

2. *Affiliate Marketing and Sales*

If you already own a website that is pulling in targeted traffic, a great method of making passive income from the content you are creating already as a side hustle idea is via affiliate marketing.

There are many affiliate tools and networks that can aid you in making cash from the content you have created already, which, in turn, enhances the income from your side hustle.

Let's take a look at some of these platforms for affiliate marketing below:

Kinds of Affiliate Networks

There is a range of affiliate networks you can exploit including a host of them which are aggregators or provide you the capacity to engage in selling the products of numerous organizations. Below are the most popular of these platforms:

- Amazon: Except you become a seller of really high-volume, the commission you earn is just 4 percent. If you use this affiliate network, you will be able to promote audiobooks, clothing, car parts, and even kitchen tools.

- Rakuten (www.rakuten.com): This was formally

recognized as Linkshare. It is a part if the aggregators that were previously mentioned. It provides the capacity to promote the product of a range of companies which includes Starbucks, iTunes, and Walmart. The amount of Walmart products you will be able to promote is in the thousands.

- Clickbank (www.clickbank.com): This website provides huge appealing commissions. This is because it has to do with the sales of information products which includes guides on transforming how to use a fitness system, alongside recipe books. For years, its primary product was information that had to do with earning cash on the web. However, it has now diverted to consist of lots of other kinds of information. This platform also provides you with advice as to the kind of products you would be able to promote online with high demand.

- JVZoo (https://www.jvzoo.com): This platform has to do with the sales of information products that have to do with earning cash online. For example, a few of its past most-recognized products have been Onesoci Platinum and WP Fan Machine. If you promote these products to marketers on the internet, it may not be a niche as broad as sales from Walmart. However, it can be just as profitable.

- Shareasale (https://www.shareasale.com/): This platform provides the chance to promote products of over 3,000 diverse organizations. Lots of them are less important specialty kind of companies like Eco Lunchbox and One Kings Lane. There is a market for all these products which implies you can earn cash if you work with Shareasale.

You Can Work with More Than One

Another great aspect of affiliate marketing is that it is not compulsory for you to work with only one of these organizations. You will be able to work with both Amazon and Shareasale and select only products from both that you would like to promote and develop an ideal store.

3. Become a Virtual Assistant

If you have a love for remaining organized or you can do numerous things, then you should try being a virtual assistant as a side hustle. You will be able to find amazing gigs on websites such as Upwork or Fiverr.

It can be a great method of relating with some very crucial individuals, developing your professional network, and acquiring new skills presently in demand like developing VR videos and GIFs. Develop your side hustle idea, and you will possess the additional benefit of being able to begin this business idea during your spare time.

Becoming a virtual assistant is a very great side hustle idea if you have plans to make additional income after the closing hours of your full-time job.

4. Remote English Tutor

Tutoring and teaching English as an additional language is an amazing side hustle. It opens doors for you to explore other parts of the world if you want. Although English as a Second Language or ESL accreditation is crucial, so long as you are an English native speaker, there are individuals in numerous countries like UAE and China who would pay you more than $20/hour for you to tutor them English through Skype.

Learn4Good, Indeed, and Remote.co often posts remote

English tutoring gigs. The instant you get that remote job, you will require a more professional environment as opposed to your dining room where you can teach students. The great part about this side hustle is that you will be able to pick up only jobs that you can tailor to your schedule.

5. Social Media Manager

Lots of us enjoy spending a decent part of our days going through Twitter, Facebook, and Instagram among others. So, why not get paid for doing these things we love? Numerous organizations, especially those just beginning in travel and retail, as well as influencers have huge presences on social media and are continuously in search of individuals with this skill. Even influencers with huge presences on social media are continually searching for people who can aid them in building their brands online.

You will be able to find these kinds of openings on websites like CareerBuilder and Flexjobs. The majority of the employers on these sites prefer working with individuals who offer these services as their side hustle. Going forward, you will be able to include more offerings like hosting profitable sweepstakes competitions and running Facebook Ad campaigns with high returns.

Once you develop your social following and develop a personal brand of your own, numerous opportunities will come your way, and you will be able to transform this side hustle into a full-time gig.

6. Google Ad Specialist

If you are conversant with paid internet marketing and can find your way around Google, a great method of earning extra funds as a side hustle is to sign a freelance contract to manage the Google Ad campaigns of a company and start to bring in more clients gradually as your consulting business develops.

Just be certain to get yourself up to date on all the appropriate industry jargon and business slangs you will be dealing with in the world of online marketing before launching yourself into this side hustle.

7. Landing Page Expert

If you are a word artisan and know how to create beautifully structured, keyword-friendly landing pages which are SEO-optimized, why not turn this into a side hustle by charging other organizations for your services?

Even a short landing page is worth a decent amount of cash in the right situation, and if you have an understanding of how to do a great pitch, you will make much more.

Interior Design Consultant.

Lots of individuals remodel various aspects of homes daily and would need help on deciding the shades that match. These people would usually be more than willing to offer you a decent amount of cash for your advice.

8. Sell Stuff on Etsy

Are you talented at creating or crafting other handmade items ranging from rings, to phone cases, to furniture? If yes, Etsy is one of the largest independent marketplaces on the globe. It is ideal for any creative individual who does not mind selling things they created with their hands.

As long as you have ample space, this could be one of the best side hustles you can begin with just a little investment. The first step is to develop your brand and your audience. The instant you have been able to get this sorted, you can begin an e-commerce website and hold on to a bigger part of the earning from the sales of your product. This can transform into a very profitable side hustle especially if you can locate an audience that enjoys your products.

9. Sell Items on eBay

Just like selling on Amazon, eBay is a platform where you can earn cash from selling almost anything that crosses your mind. This, coupled with the additional excitement of utilizing the auction-selling model to get much more than you anticipated for an item you got at a local street fair, makes this a great platform.

To transform your sales on eBay into a profitable side hustle, search for openings where you can purchase in-demand items at a lower price and sell them for more. Later on, you can use the lessons you attained from your store on eBay to develop a full e-commerce business or blog.

10. Fiverr Gigs

Fiverr is an amazing location for freelancers who have just begun and may not have lots of experience but desire to develop a work portfolio. You will have the capacity to finish easy tasks such as creating animations or logo designs.

How Do You Earn on Fiverr?

How would you be able to make cash charging only five dollars for each project?

One great thing about Fiverr is the fact that it eradicates price negotiation or haggling. You will be able to sell any service for five dollars each. So, how do you earn cash doing this? The idea behind earning cash on Fiverr is speed. If you need five hours to develop a great logo, then Fiverr may not be a great choice for you.

You need to have the capacity to do about 4 or more gigs every hour. This way, as opposed to earning only five dollars, you will be able to earn anything from $20 and above every hour.

The next step for earning cash on Fiverr is by augmenting the services you provide. Your primary service could be the creation of logos, but you may have other services which can aid you in charging an additional amount.

You may also offer one free revision but change an extra $5 or more to make additional revisions. Individuals who have attained success on Fiverr state that you need to select and learn a service, then build yourself up with the skills crucial for its delivery.

You need to be aware of your target market and reach it utilizing all the possible means of promoting your Gig.

Although this side hustle may not make you a million dollars at the start, it could still act as a platform for getting the funds you need for your subsequent business idea. This is possible if you become a top-rated seller and get some recurrent sales.

11. Online Dating Consultant

This may be hard to believe, but some individuals have difficulty in dating to the extent that they don't want to partake in the app-based part of it. If you are great with words, why not take advantage of this skill into becoming a matchmaker who gets paid to do it. Lots of these individuals would gladly pay you for this service.

12. Consultant for a WordPress Website

Numerous small businesses begin their presence on the web with a website hosted by WordPress before having to move to other comprehensive solutions for a host of reasons.

Lots of them will pay a huge amount of cash for an individual to help them set up their business idea on the web. If you are patient to learn how to do it on your own, it is a very valuable skill that you can transform into a side hustle. This is the case especially if you sign up for affiliate programs with organizations like Kinsta, who provides properly-managed WordPress hosting plans that let you attain fees from the customers you direct to them.

Also, with the skills you attain from this side hustle, you will have the capacity to create other valuable website ideas, which would bring you a decent income.

13. Create an Application

Sometimes, it may feel that there is an application for everything. However, new ones seem to crop up daily and sell for lots of cash every time. If you locate a niche that has not been occupied to its potential, and you can learn the coding skills or know a person who has them already, this could be a great business idea to leverage on. Now, you can even build an app with any skills in coding at all. Just ensure your app idea is validated before you go too far.

Even if your application does not become a top-selling one, you will be able to amass valuable skills.

14. Online News Correspondent

These days, to be a reporter, a degree in journalism is not required. Also, numerous news sites always require a little help in attaining coverage around you. Websites like HuffPost or The Examiner will offer distributors compensation based on the ad revenue amassed for every article written, which makes it an amazing incentive to offer captivating content to news companies as your side hustle.

15. Patent an Item

This is not a side hustle suitable for lots of individuals. However, you don't need to invent a flying chair before you can make great cash from your patented ideas. Just ensure that you can affordably produce the idea, so that you do not need to face a lawsuit later on.

16. Purchase and Sales of Domain Names

Trading domain names has existed for a while, and while lots of popular names have already been sold, there is still a host of others you can get for a low price and broker as your side hustle.

However, note that a few professionals doubt the longevity of this business hustle, so ensure you don't resign from your full-time job just to invest all your time into this.

17. Freelance Editing and Proofreading

As long as written content still exists, editors will equally exist as well. Freelance proofreading and editing not only pays a reasonable hourly income, but can also offer you the chance to read about possibly appealing topics as well. Also, pursuing business in freelance editing and writing can provide a lifestyle that allows you to travel the globe as a digital expert.

You will be able to locate numerous job openings from individuals and organizations that require editing, proofreading, and writing services on Upwork, which makes this a side hustle a highly-demanded one.

18. Become a Data Analyst

Do you have a knack for numbers? Lots of organizations need to hire contractors who are talented and great at data analysis. This makes it a possibly viable side hustle idea if you have the appropriate experience and credentials.

Platforms like Digiserved and Upwork are two of numerous sites that are ideal for freelancers who are great at analytics and in search of additional work that they can do in their spare time.

19. Freelance Copywriting and Writing

Most website owners get the services of copywriters to write content for pages like FAQ, about pages, and blog posts. Novice copywriters do not get very high hourly wages, but with a bit of experience and an increasing portfolio, you will be able to become a freelance writer today, and soon, you will be charging more than you earn at your full-time gig if you locate the appropriate clients and position yourself as a professional. Later on, you can advance to cold calling clients to offer your services to them.

20. Fill Out Surveys Online

Online surveys although not mentally stimulating or engaging can make you a decent amount of cash as a side hustle. Some companies are willing to pay you cash to complete surveys like Survey Junkie. Some other sites like Swagbucks pay well even if it is done in the form of Amazon gift cards.

You can do surveys during your spare time and earn a little extra cash along with it.

21. Begin a Channel on YouTube

If you love spending time on YouTube, you can create a viable side hustle from this if you do it seriously. If you can develop entertaining, value-driven content and develop your viewer and subscriber base to a reasonable amount, your videos can begin to generate a decent amount of income from the ads being shown in your videos.

Lots of YouTube users make lots of cash every year, so there is a lot of potential to take this side hustle into a high-paying business with the proper combination of skills, timing, content, audience, and relationships.

If you are considering beginning a channel on YouTube, it is crucial to utilize the leading practices when creating videos. You also need to consider investing in a quality microphone and camera since the quality of production can often have a direct impact on your viewership.

22. Try Ghostwriting

Ghostwriting brings lots of cash. If you are proficient at doing research and developing amazing content in a specific niche, you can rapidly develop a high-paying customer base with this side hustle. Lots of ghostwriters have established very profitable businesses for themselves by writing for CEO's and business executives.

It takes a lot of work to get to the position where you begin to earn full-time income off ghostwriting, but if you persevere, and rise after each fall, you are certain to be successful.

23. Subcontracting Online

The instant you have become reputable in a range of freelance verticals on the web, you can spend time on making inside sales like booking freelance contracts with high-paying clients. Then you subcontract the jobs to other freelancers. This way, you will be able to develop your clientele while amassing revenue with this side hustle.

24. Freelance Content Marketing

Startups, important influencers, and even established brands will always have the need to develop credibility and their brands. Experts who can always provide captivating content always benefit from massive demand for their services. Also, because brands will always require high quality content to draw in new clients, your skills will always be an essential asset to invest in since content marketing strategy is ever-changing.

Begin by taking advantage of the network you already have with this side hustle and start to locate owners of small businesses which would find your marketing tactics significant. Do a great job, request for referrals, and develop from there to where you will be able to spread to a broader market.

25. Freelance eBook Writer

If you have always had the desire to publish a book of your own as a side hustle, there is no better time than now to begin. This is because accessing self-publishing marketplaces and tools has never been more affordable and more accessible.

Presently, some eBook writers earn a lot of money from eBooks while focusing on their full-time jobs.

26. Developing a Niche Site

If you can locate an audience for your hobby or passion, you will be ready to monetize something you enjoy through a niche site as a side hustle. It is easier said than done and it is not something that is ideal for just anyone.

You need to be ready to input lots of time, but if you can deal with the possible setbacks and provide definite answers for some crucial questions such as if the website you want to consider starting is profitable before you start developing it.

27.   Buying an Existing Website

Websites share a lot of similarities with stock. A few of them are useless, but others can aid in generating value on your behalf which makes it a great side hustle if you know how to spot the diamond in the stack. For this reason, just like stocks, these are purchased and sold every time.

You can purchase and sell websites as a side hustle in the hopes of generating earnings in future, based on the present intake of revenue, domain name, and a host of other factors that may be a hidden source of income other people may not have seen.

If this is a side hustle that interests you, take a look at marketplaces like Flipping Enterprises and Flippa.

28.   Transcription of Interviews

Journalist and writers of nonfiction often end up recording numerous hours of interviews but don't have the necessary time to transcribe them. Now, with the help of the internet, these individuals will be able to just send the digital file of their audio interviews via emails to people like you. All you have to do is listen, type them out, and send it back via email.

Required Skills

If you want to earn cash from transcribing interviews, you would require a stable internet connection. You should equally have the capacity to accurately and quickly type and have a great pair of headsets as it will make it easier for you to understand the interviews.

You will also require a degree of patience because a few interviews can be tedious to understand, and you may need to head back and listen to specific sections multiple times to understand what is being said. The harsh truth is that some individuals are not very eloquent, have the tendency to mumble and rush their responses. If you are an individual who becomes frustrated often, then this may not be a side hustle for you.

Expected Earning

Depending on your typing speed and the type of assignments, you would be able to earn around $5 to as much as $50 every hour. The website VerbalInk offers new transcribers $1.50 every minute. In essence, transcribing an interview of 20-minutes will earn you $30. It will also pay you more if there are numerous individuals taking part in the interview, if there is heavy noise at the background, or if one or more individuals in the interview have a great accent.

Where You Can Find Work

Asides from Verbalink, you can also check out Scribe which emphasizes on the field of medicine. You can also check out Upwork for work. One of the leading aspects of transcribing interviews is the fact that you can work as little or as much as you desire. Some individuals do this as a part-time side hustle to support their normal income while others do it as a full-time income. You would also have the capacity to get work by reaching out to a local TV station that transmits lots of news alongside newspapers and magazines.

If you want to take this further, you can have a look at the websites of book authors and publishers and search for mailing addresses and links of those authors and offer them your services.

29. Make Cash by Sharing Your Thoughts

You most likely have opinions about a range of various things. But are you aware that you could make money just by sharing your opinions? While you may not be a billionaire from this, you could make a reasonable amount of side income which requires only a little portion of your time.

There are a few websites in search of the opinions of individuals which includes:

Swagbucks

This is a platform which offers you payment in the form of rewards and gift cards for taking surveys, watching videos, and shopping at your best stores among a host of others. This platform has offered its members over $100M, and it does not cost anything to join. You will only be doing the things you usually do on the web which consists of answering polls, shopping, surfing the web, and playing games. After doing this, you will gather points that can be redeemed via your desired gift cards. Additionally, you will be able to invite friends and complete special offers.

Opinion Outpost

This has more focus than Swagbucks as it provides rewards and cash when you answer online surveys. It also has to do with you accumulating points after completing surveys which you will be able to redeem for a gift or cash vouchers to well-known brands. Signing up on this platform is free, and the instant you do so, you will be privy to receiving payment to complete surveys relating to topics such as sports, appliances, or medicine.

You get paid for this because your opinion is valued by companies and will offer you rewards when you share them. This platform offers you two choices for participating which could be by logging into its site or by email. It is different from other survey companies as it provides a quarterly prize draw which can get to as high as $10,000.

30.   Be a Seller on Teespring

T-shirts can be a profitable path to developing a side hustle that earns you cash while you sleep. TeeSpring is another platform that can help you do just this.

Utilize Email and Social Media

It would be amazing if your t-shirts were able to sell themselves, but this is hardly ever the case. You would have to notify your friends and family members about your design using social media and email. If you are targeting a niche market, you could purchase some ads. While your clients will purchase your t-shirts, they won't be charged until your campaign gets its sales objective.

How Do You Make Money Via Teespring?

On Teespring, there is an aspect titled Teeview where you will be able to see the present campaigns on TeeSprings. You can also check it out to see the shirts selling. You will be able to sort campaigns using a number of sales or look for that which is more viable. Most importantly, ensure your design is simple and if you can, take advantage of a new trend.

What this implies is that you design shirts around trending topics which could be popular celebrities, TV shows, or sporting events. If you are not an experienced designer, don't make any effort to develop a design by yourself. Hire the services of a designer on Upwork or Fiverr to develop your design. It is ideal to have some color and style options to enable your clients to select their best choice. When you are just beginning, ensure that your goal for sales is not too high. If you have minimal or no traffic and not much cash for advertising, aim for lesser numbers like 5-10 as it would work perfectly, and it is a target you should be able to attain.

31. Create Custom Software for Clients

Software is valuable in businesses today. It is a known fact that companies and individuals are making efforts to make a name for themselves, earn profits, or just get things done. Due to this, there would be much more prospects for software developers as opposed to other jobs. This would create huge opportunities for this side hustle further into the future.

In fact, it won't take you much time to get a software development project with good pat as a side hustle on platforms like Freelancer, Guru.com, and Upwork. Even LinkedIn launched their recent freelancing brand, known as ProFinder, which has a section dedicated solely for hiring great software developers.

32. Voice-Over Artist

If you have a great and unique voice, a range of digital publishers including training video creators, animated film-producers, and game developers will pay you a decent amount of cash for voice talent. It does not require too much time which makes it an amazing side hustle.

You will be able to locate publishers searching for voice-over artists on websites like Freelancer, PeoplePerHour, and

Upwork as well as their requests for talent straight on their sites or via voiceover agents. If you do go with this side hustle, be ready for the long-haul as this can be an industry with a lot of competition

33. Develop an Extension for Chrome

With over 50,000 paid and free custom extensions in Google Chrome's market place, there is large opportunity to develop a useful extension for individuals to utilize while going through the internet as a business idea which requires minimal effort.

There are numerous extensions for different purposes on chrome. You are certain to find a need that you can fill in with an extension. This side hustle is especially ideal because it lets you showcase your skills in development. A great part about this is that aside from launching chrome extensions, you can also do it on a freelance basis.

34. Brand Ambassador

It may seem unbelievable, but it is possible to earn cash from representing your favorite brands at events across the globe. If you have an outgoing and friendly personality and perhaps a decent social media following, you will be able to forge a relationship as a brand ambassador with organizations who need to reach people in your environment. This is a side hustle that has the potential to bring in a decent amount of cash.

As the ambassador of a brand, you can do things ranging from showcasing recent technology to going around the world on tours to giving free stuff at music festivals.

Based on the gig, you will be able to make anything from $20-$100 every hour. You will be able to easily begin this side hustle by becoming a member of the Brand Ambassador Facebook group for your closest major city.

The instant you have gotten approval to be a member of the group, you will be provided access to job postings from large agencies and brands with openings in your area daily. All you have to do is send in your headshot and resume to apply.

Chapter 5: More Side Hustle Ideas

If you are not partial to online side hustles and would prefer something more hands-on, there are a lot of choices available to you.

Below are a few of them:

1. Be a Photographer

If you are the owner of a camera who loves pictures, beginning a freelance photography business is a great way of transforming your passions and skills into a profitable side hustle.

Begin by doing shoots for your family and friends for free to develop a great portfolio online. Familiarize yourself with your editing process and gear, so that you will have the capacity to earn cash from taking pictures of great family moments. Also, the instant you have all your photography gear, you will be able to earn some more at the side by renting it out when you are not utilizing it via marketplaces online like Fat Lama.

Once you have mastered your skills, you can go further into taking pictures at weddings. After all, taking great pictures is one of the most crucial life moments of people which makes it a very profitable side hustle.

Do Stock Photography

If you are fond of taking beautiful pictures of laughing kids or smiling families, why not try going into stock photography? You can sell your pictures to a stock image organization like Shutterstock, Unsplash, and iStockPhoto.

Each time an individual licenses an image you send in, you will be offered royalties. To further attain success, develop your photography side to allow you to display your work, and begin attaining corporate work for higher pay.

2. Writing Greeting Cards and Erotic Stories

The demand for fiction is on the high side. As strange as this may sound, if you have a great imagination, you can make more than $2,000 each month writing erotic fiction in your spare time as a side hustle.

The same applies if you are a great poet. You can make $200 or more for each poem you write published by greeting card companies. If you are amazing with words and can handle rejections which you may face initially, this may be a great fit for you.

3. Sales of Phone Case

There is a large rising market for mobile phone accessories, and lots of handmade sellers are raking in large amounts of cash from their business of selling phone cases. You will be able to begin your own phone case business instantly in a few days.

The instant you have begun, you will be able to sell these cases on Fancy, Amazon Handmade, and Etsy. You can also make extra sales from promotional product vendors, events, parties, trade shows, and other marketplaces online. With time, your sales would grow, and you would be able to transform this side hustle into a full-time business.

4. Earn Commission from Sales

If you can connect with individuals and take risks, going into freelance sales based on commission can be an amazing side hustle idea for you. Lots of start-ups are always in search of salespeople who will only work part-time and get paid on commission. This is the case especially when they are just kicking off. What this means is you will be able to make this an idea you can do in your spare time.

Create your sales strategies, become a sales rep, and enhance your cold-calling skills in your spare time for just commissions. Negotiate some equity, and you would be able to make a huge profit if you are trying to pitch a great product, and the startup is successful.

You can begin your sales education using bestselling books from Daniel Pink like To Sell is Human among others, and you will be heading to kick-starting this side business hustle.

Then you can head on to more engaging sales education via online courses on Udemy and CreativeLive. The instant you are ready to try out your selling skills, take a look at Angel list for any sales opportunities that go with your interests. You do not want to get stuck selling services or products you have no interest in.

By beginning your career in sales as a side hustle, it would offer you the flexibility to change courses with ease if the need comes up.

5. Preparing Tax

This is not an easy side business, but someone has to ensure that at the end of the year, all the numbers add up. Most individuals and organizations, especially resource and time-strapped business owners require someone that has the expertise to aid in the preparation of tax returns.

There are courses on Udemy that can help you with this, and in a few hours of practice and training, you will have upgraded your skills in preparing tax returns.

6. SAT Tutor

If you have a proficiency for standardized tests and had no issues acing the ACT, SAT, or other college exams people tend to have issues with, why don't you begin to tutor high school students? Parents from all areas and financial status would be more than willing to offer more than $50/hour for the appropriate tutor if it means that it would help their kids get into the university or college they desire.

7. Presentation Design Consultant

Sometimes, even PowerPoint presentations need external consulting especially if it is not your field. Lots of companies will gladly pay an expert to do their presentation decks for lectures and investor pitches.

This is a skill you can transform into a side hustle business and earn as much as $15 or more for each slide you create.

8. Travel Consultant

If you enjoy traveling and notice yourself looking for airfare sales or other travel websites, why not create a niche of your own as a private travel agent. Begin with recommendations from your loved ones and friends who are certain that they can depend on you for the least expensive flights.

Develop a LinkedIn or Facebook group for those who desire to stay abreast with the most recent deals, and eventually, you could transform this side hustle into a full-time business of teaching individuals how to make their dream trip come true.

9. Housesitting

This may not make your regular income, but this is an amazing business hustle. If you have a flexible full-time job, you will be able to do this in your spare time and live in various locations free of charge while making income.

10. Babysitting

If you love children, then babysitting on weekends and nights is a great way to earn more cash. Depending on your residence and the kind of job, you may earn as much as $20 every hour to watch the kids of other individuals. You will have to be ready to let go of a huge part of your personal time if you want to earn a decent amount of cash here.

Babysitting is not difficult, and it is not just for college students and teenagers as goes the popular belief. Also, note that a few families will require you to get a CPR certification before they hire you. If you do not have it, you only need to complete an affordable and short course to get it. This is a side hustle idea that would help you rake in a reasonable amount of cash if you work weekends and nights if the odd hours do not bother you.

11. Manager of Properties

If you know a person who rents his property to other people, then they would likely use your help in the management of their property. If this is the case, you can make a reasonable amount of cash doing the side hustle with only a bit of work from your end.

It will require some willingness to make changes to your schedule on a whim and a bit of hustling. This is because you will be charged with the responsibility of managing repairs, collecting rent checks, and simply being available for emergencies. However, a property manager is crucial for the majority of the real estate investors that have a huge portfolio, so this business idea certainly comes with some benefits.

12. Editor of College Admissions Essay

If editing and offering advice to college students on ways to write captivating essays on various topics seems like an appealing side hustle to you, then you are on the right path. Numerous parents will let go of a decent amount of cash for you to edit an admission essay and provide their children with constructive feedback.

All you need to ensure is that you don't write their essays for them, but play the role of an editor to aid them in getting their message across. This can transform into an amazing business idea that has the possibility of spreading by word of mouth referrals in your environment.

13. Purchase Used Electronics, Overhaul, and Sell Them

Lots of individuals abandon their faulty mobile phones, cameras, and laptops without even making efforts to find the reason they malfunctioned in the first place. If you possess the skills to repair them, why not make this a side hustle? You can refurbish these items and resell them later on during your free time.

14. Be a "Looker."

Do you know you can earn cash just by heading to look at something? Well, this is possible with the help of the website: WeGoLook. It has over 10,000 lookers, many of which include retired veterans, process servers, and school teachers among others in search of ways to earn additional income in the sharing and crowdsourcing economy today.

How Does It Work?

This platform operates in a very simple manner. You head to the website to complete an application where you would have to pass a background check and get the mobile app for the platform.

When you are given a task, you will be required to dress in a professional manner, and you need to be friendly when working with clients and have the capacity to carry out the Looks via your smartphone.

When you come across a job on the application, you have to be the first to request it. Generally, you will be offered the location of the property or item involved alongside the owner or seller's contact details, who will be expecting you to reach out.

You will make contact quickly, and set up a meeting. The instant you are there, you will take some pictures, and answer some easy questions on a checklist. Then you will upload the images and finish a brief report on the website.

You will have the capacity to earn anything from $20 to over $200. An example of something you will be asked to look at is a home or apartment to take videos of for an out of town renter or buyer.

Expected Earnings

Similar to most gigs, the answer to this is relative. It is dependent on the number of tasks you can get and when they pay. Sadly, these are outcomes you can't control. If you are lucky and fast, you may be able to clinch five looks a week at $30 each for a total of $150 –just to look at things and report about them. This is a great side hustle that you can do during your spare time and make a decent amount of extra income.

15. Begin a Popup Shop

While the hindrances to enter a retail shop are a lot, one method of keeping down costs and limiting the time you invest while retaining your full-time source of income is to begin a popup shop during the weekend.

The majority of whatever you earn by selling things such as clothing, snacks, or any other stuff will remain in your pockets as opposed to paying for operating costs like utilities or rents by deciding to chase retail with a short-term rental. Check out this Shopify glide for a step-by-step process of beginning your popup shop.

16. Brew Beer

Do you love to drink beer? If yes, why not try creating it yourself? With adequate skill and patience, you may be able to brew something that others will want to pay for and drink. Search for a starter kit online that is easy to utilize like Mr. Beer and invest the time it will require to make your craft perfect, create a distinct brew, and begin to distribute it around to family and friends to see what they feel about this side hustle.

17. Drive for Uber or Lyft

Drive for one of the two internationally growing alternative taxi services which are app-centric. Lyft and Uber can still be a decently profitable method of earning cash as a side business during the weekends and at night. You will be able to work only when you want.

However, before heading into this side hustle idea, you need to research and calculate the costs of tires, mileage, extra gas, and wear and tear of your car. It is not a business idea that is certain to provide you with profit each weekend.

There have been reports that Lyft drivers earn around $12-17 every hour. Create your account and head to the application whenever you have spare time and need to earn some additional income. If you observe that you are a fan of driving, you will earn a bonus of $250 after your initial 100 rides on Lyft, and you will be able to keep all the tips you earn.

18. Rent Out Your Vehicle on Turo

If you own a vehicle that you hardly use, you can earn some cash on the side by renting it on Turo. For more confidence, there is an insurance policy on all vehicles worth $1 Million and drivers go through major prescreening.

19. Collector of Arts

Not to be mixed up with hoarding, this is a side hustle which requires lots of patience, time, and passion. If you have a great eye for amazing art, you can kick this off by paying a visit to the studio department at the university in your locality. However, you have to note that you may not make millions from this side hustle. Lots of art students are comfortable selling their work after negotiation, and in just a few years, there is a huge possibility that a piece you purchased for a little cash may have a worth of over thousands. Note that this business hustle is one that will require a huge amount of patience and vast space for storing art.

20. Catering

Are you a great cook whose meals friends and family tend to love? Then why not transform it into a side hustle? A great way to tryout being a chef is to use EatWith. If you have adequate rave reviews, you may be able to transform your cooking skills into a full-time gig where you will be taking advantage of your network to get catering jobs.

This side hustle is heavily dependent on attaining satisfied referrals, so be certain you over-deliver for your initial clients, and ask if they know other individuals who may require your catering services.

21. Purchase Parts from Electronics Stores

It may be unbelievable, but there may be lots of cash to earn from valuable items being disposed of by large stores around the globe. Large electronic stores throw out various items ranging from tablets to printer cartridges.

If you have the stomach to search around dumpsters, you will have the capacity to earn a decent amount of cash this way.

22. Licensed Distributor of Products

It may not happen in one day, but licensing an imported product which you can sell domestically can be a viable side hustle that sometimes results in a large payoff in the future. If you make smart investments and sell products you believe in, you will be able to reap the benefit for numerous years in the future.

23. Consulting for Local Businesses

If you have amassed valuable sets of certifications or skills within your sector over the years, you can consider taking advantage of these skills during your free time by providing your consulting services to owners of local businesses as a potentially lucrative business.

Irrespective of if you are a business strategist, professional marketer, or expert in other fields, then there are certainly business owners who would want to offer you payment to aid them in solving a problem with their organization as long as you can produce an efficient cold mail that urges them to hire you. This is a business idea you can take advantage of and begin today.

24. Sell Your Old Books

Lots of homes have numerous books lying around amassing dust. So, why not transform them into money? Websites like Bookscouter will aid you in selling them at the highest price possible. It works by comparing prices from numerous websites that do with the sales of books so you can almost instantly locate who would pay the highest for your books. Yes, book prices often change and can differ greatly among buyers so comparing book buyers utilizing a range of criteria can be helpful. This will aid you in determining where you will be able to sell your books at the ideal price.

Sell the Books of Others

If you don't possess books of your own, then one of the least difficult things to find at an estate, garage, and yard sales is books. The individuals who are disposing of them usually don't know their actual value. One of the best methods of selling books via a website like Bookscouter is to be a specialist in a unique category like historical fiction, mysteries, children's books, and romance novels.

Do this, and you will be aware of the value of books and the amount to pay for them which will still ensure you earn a profit. In numerous situations, you will be able to find books at giveaway prices at an estate and yard sales because individuals want to dispose of them. You may end up buying books for only $1-2 to find out they are worth 10$ or more.

One of the great aspects of BookScouter is that you don't need to register, and it does not cost anything to use. But, if you believe you will be selling numerous books, you can get an upgrade known as BookScouter Pro which needs a monthly subscription and also offers you with tracking, book lookup tool, and uninterrupted usage among a host of other tools.

Do You Own Textbooks?

If you have kids who have been in college or are currently attending, then you must be aware of how expensive textbooks can be. BookScouter can be an ideal location for the sales of used textbooks. People are earning more than $200 monthly just by selling textbooks, and it is not difficult.

All you have to do is put in the ISBN of the book in BookScouter. You will then be able to select the leading offer for the book and send it to the reseller. Resellers on BookScouts typically pay by check or PayPal.

Things to Note

BookScouter has some downsides. For one, it does not share guidelines as to what would be a book's acceptable condition. As opposed to this, it directs you to the website of the reseller where you will need to search for suitable conditions. This is crucial because if you transfer a book to the reseller which he does not find acceptable, you will fail to receive payment for it.

Another drawback is that, as stated by BookScouter itself, it isn't a good location for the sales of rare, collectible, and antique books which has the possibility of earning you higher cash in other places.

25. Be a Field Agent

Here, you will earn cash for doing various jobs for clients of www.gigwalk.com. The business plan of companies like this is to link clients with individuals to do small jobs in their vicinity, like taking a picture of the display in a store.

You will earn cash by completing the assigned jobs for the organization.

What Would You Be Doing?

Field agents may collect numerous kinds of information. In some situations, you may need to take pictures that would be utilized in the verification of information, capturing how products are utilized or the in-store experiences of individuals. You may also have the job of collecting opinions and performing surveys.

For data assignments, field agents basically utilize methodology for data collection coupled with technology like scanning the barcode to ensure data quality. By working as a field agent for any of these sites, you may also have the job of getting feedback from the primary customers on services at the areas of influence.

How Do You Begin?

If you want to become a field agent as a side hustle, the first thing you have to do is to download the Field Agent Application. Then, you would complete your profile where you will be asked to answer some basic questions.

The organization points out that you have to accurately complete the questions as this is crucial to ensuring you see the appropriate jobs in your area and system. On the core navigation window in the Field Agent Application, you will find the job lists. This is where you will search for jobs or tasks that you find interesting. The instant you pick a job, you will be provided with 2 hours to complete it. This means you have to ensure you are close to the target point before accepting the task.

Earning Potential

Generally, jobs on Field Agent pay around $2 - $12 per job depending on the kind of task you are asked to do.

26. Airbnb Host

Do you have a spare room or an entire home you have nothing to do with? If yes, then Airbnb is a great choice for you. It is an amazing way of making cash by renting out your living room couch or extra bedroom to people. You will also enjoy the benefit of getting to meet new individuals and making new acquaintances or friends if you are open to it.

You will be able to rent out your complete new apartment and manage via Airbnb as a side hustle. However, this may not be a passive income source, you will be on call anytime there is a guest, and you will always have to ensure the place is kept tidy for incoming guests. Asides from just renting your space on Airbnb, you can equally take the idea to the next step by providing your visitors with personalized experiences for an additional charge.

27. Personal Fitness Trainer

If you are into fitness and have the appropriate blend of business sense and charisma, being a part-time trainer during your spare time can be both financially and physically beneficial. The instant you have developed a client base and reputation for yourself, you could turn it into a full-time business for yourself.

28. Meditation or Yoga Instructor

Yoga is gaining popularity which implies demand for yoga instructors is on the rise, making it another appealing profitable side hustle. Reach out to a local yoga studio to take night classes or provide in-house yoga services for more money to chase this form of physical and emotional balance during your spare time while increasing your account balance as well.

29. Become a Translator

If your knowledge of another language is proficient enough to have the spelling and grammar down, translation is an amazing side hustle to try out, and you can do it in your spare time. You can find numerous remote translator and freelance jobs on Flexjobs which you can use to earn extra cash.

30. Be a Tour Guide

Do you reside in a destination frequented by travelers? If you enjoy meeting new individuals around the globe and love your city of residence, beginning your local tour organization is one of the best side hustles that will offer you a chance to make use of both of these interests.

31. Music Instructor

Are you conversant with a specific musical instrument enough to tutor others? How about using your skills at creating a sound design or music and teaching other people based on your experience? Private music instructors in all fields charge around $20 or more every hour depending on experience and skill. It makes for an amazing business idea which you can use in transforming your music passion into profit.

32. Become a DJ

Take the time to hone your skills at either developing your music or becoming an expert in mixing. Once you can do this, your side hustle of being a DJ at local events could transform into a more profitable venture.

You will first have to command a comprehensive knowledge of music production, sound design, and mixing before you expect to get your first gig with this business idea. This is because developing a whole new skill set is not entirely easy.

33. Alterations of Clothing and Tailoring

Style, fashion, and grooming remain side hustles that you can do after work. If you have a knowledge of mending clothes, then you have an increasing market of customers who are conscious of their budget or obsessed with personalization.

34. Teaching DIYs

Nothing is better than teaching more novice individuals about your hobby, craft, or passion as a side hustle. Check out numerous DIY portals like DIY Network, Mahalo, and Instructables among others to attain ideas on how you can earn a reasonable amount of side income only by showing others how to do stuff you enjoy. There are also numerous ad-supported channels that you can use to learn almost anything to teach others.

35. Bake for Income

Baking can easily equate to making cash. You can bring in extra income by mastering the oven, kneading flour, and satisfying the thirst for sweet stuff that everyone has. Although some entrepreneurs are already doing baking full-time, you don't have to leave your full-time job to pursue this side hustle idea immediately.

Depending on the level of experience you have, you can begin by doing the easy stuff before trying more complex stuff.

36. Become a Task Rabbit

If you see nothing wrong in doing the chores of other

individuals, then TaskRabbit may be the ideal side hustle for you. Earn a little extra cash doing jobs like mowing your neighbor's lawn or walking dogs.

The leading taskers on the platform reportedly make as high as $6,000 and more every month, which makes this a full-time side hustle for some individuals.

37. Investing Your Cash

If you hide your cash in a bunker or in a savings account where it earns almost nothing, you may want to consider utilizing it better via smarter investing as your side hustle. Yes, there are a host of dangers to watch out for, but numerous personal finance professionals will advise you to begin learning about the stock market if you have plans to increase your wealth. They will also tell you to stay away from diving too deeply into trends like cryptocurrencies without adequate understanding.

38. Investing the Money of Others

Assisting other individuals in developing their wealth is also a fantastic way of growing your finance as a side hustle. If you have finance and stock market credentials, you will be able to earn consulting fees or commissions by advising clients on the way they can get the top returns for their investments. This can be a profitable side hustle if you can provide your clients with the best results or else, this side hustle is a fast way of losing family and friends, so you need to exercise caution.

39. Bookkeeping and Accounting

Lots of start-ups and small organizations are now outsourcing jobs that are not included in their primary business. It makes this skill a chance to begin a side hustle that engages your prowess in numbers.

Because organizations always need to monitor the flow of cash, freelance bookkeepers and accountants can benefit from the rising demand for part-time assistance.

40. Car Detailing and Washing

Numerous vehicle owners do not have time to care for their cars personally, talk more of making them shine. With simple equipment like tire black, polishing wax, car shampoo among others, you can begin to earn a reasonable income on the side by making vehicles have a fresher look in your spare time after work and during weekends.

41. Caregiving

Offering care to the elderly often needs a more comprehensive set of credentials. For this reason, this is not a business idea lots of people can begin instantly. These credentials may consist of training certificates, licenses, tax forms, and business permits among others depending on the state you desire to run your operation, the level of care you plan on providing, and if you have plans to run this business full-time or do it as a side hustle.

If you are already offering unpaid care to an elderly friend or relative, you may want to check out the Medicaid provisions to find some reimbursement. In all situations, it is essential you have real love for the elderly, lots of common sense, and a vast knowledge of CPR, first aid, and basics for elderly care to prosper in this side hustle.

42. Cleaning Carpets

Carpets offer you a cozy and warm home. However, they tend to amass allergens, stains, dust, bugs, and grimes as time goes on. You will be able to take advantage of this opportunity by creating a carpet cleaning side hustle or act as an independent contract cleaner in your spare time.

Either way, you will have to invest in the appropriate equipment like carpet brushes, vacuum cleaners, and cleaning chemicals to kick-off this side hustle. Find out how possible it is to rent equipment for an entire weekend and line up a few customers to service to clear your cost of rent.

If you bring in good profit, you will have the capacity to invest in buying equipment of your own eventually and enhance your margins, thus moving this to a full-time business.

43. Cleaning Homes

If you want to expand your services and earn higher, you can choose to make the whole home look clean and neat with this business. House-cleaning services include lawns, windows, carpets, and require a broad range of tools for cleaning.

You can hire janitors or maids to carry out the actual cleaning while you deal with the administrative, sales, and customer service aspects. Also, you can begin small by doing the job yourself as a contractor, getting the ropes of the job before beginning your cleaning operation.

44. Child Care

Lots of families that have children, single parents included, have limited resources as regards time. This ensures there is a high demand for part-time providers of childcare which can be an excellent side hustle idea.

If you care about kids and have some time on your hands, you will be able to earn lots of side income by looking after kids while their parents are not home. Just be sure to pinpoint the specific age group you are okay with, and you can start after all the appropriate certifications. With the right environment, you will be able to expand this business idea into something more substantial.

45. Computer Repair

Technical experts who have plans to earn extra cash on the side can take advantage of their hardware and software skills by providing computer repair services from home.

If you fall into this category, you can start this side hustle on your own before you decide to invest more and grow your operation. Note that you will be able to offer local home service as a starting point. You could also offer remote support via video-calling services and online messaging before you head into a retail setting.

46. Modeling

If you have the look and attitude, there should be a service or product in search of the appropriate model to help in promoting their brand. You will be able to sign up with a large agency, locate a freelance agent, and search for your gigs later on.

Because the modeling sector is complicated, its best to get all the advice you require before you dive in. You can also locate a mentor who will be able to lead you through a few of the initial issues you will go through when trying to establish your brand. Depending on what you prefer, you can focus on one media format like still images or videos, develop a captivating portfolio, and develop this into a side hustle that can prosper.

47. Computer Lessons and Training

Individuals in different age ranges which include retirees and kids require some level of technical expertise to remain competitive and appreciate the wonders the digital age provides.

If you are a technical expert, you can rake in cash by providing tutorials and lessons within your environment. You can also do it via the web using platforms like Udemy or YouTube as a side hustle. You will also be able to create a tutorial website of your own which has an interface for making payments online.

48.   Contract Customer Service

There are firms which subcontract their customer service operations and lots of these organizations support contractors who are home-based. You can begin by registering on freelance websites like Fiverr and Upwork to try out this idea initially.

If you are a customer service expert that possess management skills, then you will be able to create and direct an online virtual team while engaging clients as a real customer service organization. You will also be able to offer customer service training to such individuals and teams.

49.   Dog Walker

Dogs are great animals. However, numerous owners are not always around to take them on walks. If you love canines, this is a fantastic gig that can bring you profit regularly just by taking some fantastic puppies for a walk in the park.

With lots of individuals who love pets but also have busy lives, offering dog-walking services is prosperous in lots of cities. There are applications like Wag, which connects dog walkers who want to take advantage of this business idea with owners of pets who require assistance.

50. Real Estate Sales Consultant

The real estate market is growing once more, and individuals are purchasing and selling properties in numerous locations around the globe. What this means is that there are lots of openings for experts who understand how to navigate the financial, commercial, and legal aspect of real estate to develop a stable clientele as a side hustle.

This is the case if you start scaling your sales hiring and building a team of reps working to aid you in closing more deals. If you see yourself as a professional in the topic, it would be easy to adapt. However, you will be able to earn a decent amount of extra side income as a real estate consultant. This is the case especially if you use a great CRM and understand how to persuade clients over the phone.

51. Creating Custom Furniture

Transforming your amazing hobby or craft into a revenue-generating side hustle counts easily as one of the best experiences any individual can possess since many individuals are requesting a higher level of personalization in just about any item they use. If your craft happens to be creating custom furniture, you are in luck; this is a side hustle that creates lots of room for growth.

52. Creating Handmade Jewelry

This is another great field to exploit. Lots of entrepreneurs have already earned a decent amount of cash from creating hand-made jewelry. The market is great for newcomers who know how to create captivating handmade goods. You will be able to take advantage of this side hustle during your spare time.

53. Be a Gigwalker.

Earning cash on GigWalk is similar to Task Rabbit. If you have ample free time, it can be a great side hustle. You will be able to select from a broad range of jobs to do. Although this won't make you a millionaire since the payouts tend to fall in the ranges of $2 - $100. However, if you are in search of a consistent side income, it won't do any harm to try this platform.

When you need cash, or you are bored, you are able to access the platform anywhere, and anytime using the mobile application. Also, all jobs vetted for you specifically will be close to you.

54. Appraisal of Homes

You can operate this kind of business on a part-time basis directly from your home if you have the credentials to support it. It is an ideal option if you do not want to let to go of your full-time income while making some extra cash on the side.

A college degree is not required to begin this business idea. However, you will require bankable appraiser credentials, knowledge, and an increasing network of players in the industry which includes banks, real estate agents, fellow appraisers, and brokers who will want to take advantage of your services.

55. Human Billboard

If you have nothing against exhibiting yourself in public locations and you love some extra attention, then this is a side hustle that can earn you a reasonable amount of money. For example, if you tattoo a brand logo on your shaven head for a couple of years, you can earn as high as $6,000. However, this is not a common earning opportunity. This business idea is certainly not for the weak minded and could be quite extreme for a few people; however, lots of individuals are taking advantage of it.

For a start, you can begin by holding a placard board advertising a company after your full-time job. The best part of this side hustle is that you don't have to bother with all the challenges that you have to think of in more complicated businesses.

56. Junk Removal Service

Like the familiar saying, "What is junk for someone is a treasure for another." This may not be an appealing side hustle, but you will be able to make the environment cleaner while you earn additional income.

To begin, you will probably require a decent second-hand truck alongside basic equipment such as garbage cans, shovels, and sledgehammers. All of these can help you kick off this idea.

57. Earn Cash by Testing New Products

Would you love trying new stuff and earn cash for it? You will be able to do it via the site CashCrate. It leverages on the fact that there are organizations that pay lots of cash for individuals like you to try their services and products. They also offer you the products free of charge.

How Do You Sign Up?

It is not difficult to sign up with CashCrate, and you will be provided with $1 when you do so. Aside from getting payment for trying out services and products, you will also be able to earn cash by partaking in online shopping, daily research surveys, and referring other individuals to the program.

What Is Your Earning Potential?

For example, on CashCrate, there may be two daily surveys which you could finish up and get a payment of $.80 for both. If you were to finish both of them each day, you would be able to make $50 monthly. When you partake in free offers, you can make money by requesting information on a range of services and products. The instant you sign up, you will have the capacity to view the free offers in the Members Area of the website. These offers range from website registration, brief surveys, trial products, and quizzes.

CashCrate will come with numerous diverse paid surveys and offers you will be able to select from. Payment will range anywhere from $.20 to as much as $50.

Not Every Offer Is Free

Majority of the offers you get on CashCrate do not cost anything, but some offers require that you offer your credit card details. In a situation where you need to offer this information, you will get a payout which will be more than what you invested in it. For example, you may have to pay around $20 for a product that needs you to sign up or has a handling and shipping fee of some dollars. In this situation, you will still get a reasonable amount of profit from this transaction.

As stated by CashCrate, the best method of earning cash is via referrals. It states that lots of its members make above $100 monthly using this method, and some of them attain checks above $500. These functions are similar to multi-level marketing. When you initially begin, you will get just the income you earn. As you continue signing up referrals, you will be provided a bonus each time any of them makes his or her initial $10. And it does not end here. The more referrals you accumulate, the more the cash you would earn from them as well.

58. Make Cash Renting Your Driveway or Garage

Are you aware that your garage or driveway could help you bring in cash? Well, this is not a lie. If you have space that you are not utilizing such as your garage or driveway, you will be able to list it on platforms such as Craigslist and transform it into revenue.

However, you have a possibility of earning more cash if you rent your garage space as opposed to your driveway. This is because there is more demand for it. Lots of individuals have occupied their garages with lots of items that they have no more space for one of their vehicles or more.

There are also individuals with collectible or exotic cars that have no location to park them. You could also move further than cars as there are likely a large number of individuals out there who have items to safeguard but would prefer not to utilize commercial storage. So, why not request a fee for them to safeguard these items in your space?

59. Places to List Your Parking or Garage Space

If you resided in England, you would be able to lease out your garage or driveway using the website JustPark. Here, you would possibly get some assistance in your pricing.

In the United States, a similar website is Rent My Garage. Listing your garage space as an ad is free on this website, and anytime you do so, you will get a notification via your email anytime a person posts an ad in search of garage space in your vicinity. You will also have the capacity to list your parking space or garage on Craigslist. Owners of homes in city downtown areas can offer off-street parking or garage space for $200 or above monthly or as much as $80 weekly. Naturally, rates in small town and suburban areas are less but go with the values of a local property.

If your charges are lower than the closest garage or commercial parking lot, you are most likely going to get great business. Another platform which suits this category is Storeatmyhouse. It refers to itself as "the Airbnb of self-storage." It is created for individuals that need to rent parking or storage spaces as opposed to garage space.

What is The Earning Potential?

It is quite realistic to expect that you would be able to get no less than $200 monthly when you rent half of your garage which would make over $2,000 monthly. However, this is dependent on a range of variables which include the size of the space you need to rent, your location of residence, and how limited garage space is in your city and its facilities. But, as a basic rule, you would have the capacity to earn higher if your garage space is in a central location of a massive city as opposed to if it is in a smaller town.

60. *Make Money by Being a Friend*

There used to be an old saying that you couldn't buy friendship. But, nowadays, this is possible. Rent a Friend is a platform which would pay you anything from $10 to as much as $50 every hour to be a friend to someone. Also, you will be privy to free meals and free concerts among a host of others.

What Is Rent a Friend?

This website advertises itself as a unique one where you will be able to create a free profile of your own and market your friendship. This is a website where you would get paid for renting out your friendship.

It asserts that there is a range of individuals around the globe who desire to make new friends, learn new skills, or have individuals they can go to events and activities with. This is ideal for you because these individuals are ready to pay cash for you to teach them a new skill, accommodate them, or just be friends with them.

Expected Earning

This is solely dependent on you and the amount of time you plan on spending being a friend. There have been friends earning more than $1000 weekly doing this as a full-time gig. However, friends doing it just on weekends make around $200 to $400 or more weekly. You will find an estimated income chart on the website which would provide you with a little idea of the amount you can earn.

61. Become a Public Notary

Public notaries majorly act as impartial witnesses and validators in public legal documents, mostly those that have to do with deeds, estates, affidavits, and business agreements among others.

Based on the state, a notary public who does this full-time makes an average yearly salary of $30,000 or more which makes it an amazing side hustle. You will be able to earn cash via other methods. If you are in the U.S and want to consider this side hustle, you need to take a look at the requirements and steps to begin.

62. Planning Weddings

Similar to birthdays, marriages take place all the time. This implies that you can take advantage of weddings as a consistent means of earning extra side income. Weddings usually consist of photographers, flower shops, videographers, wedding dresses, flower shops, and travel agencies.

Now just imagine if you are able to create a network of all of these service providers, so you will be able to offer couples a barrage of seamless wedding packages. This is a time-consuming and fun process which will make a great side hustle with amazing pay.

63. Become a Party Planner

For high-level players, being a wedding planner works well. But if you are a generalist, it also comes with its benefits. Party and event planners don't cover just weddings, but also corporate events, conferences, birthdays, holiday parties, and concerts among a range of others which makes this side hustle quite diverse.

There are numerous benefits and drawbacks to this side hustle, so it's best to do your research properly before delving into it.

64. Become a Personal Chef

For lots of individuals, their daily schedules can be stressful. It can also cause a disruption to the family life to the point that kids laden with homework and busy parents scarcely have time to make decent weekend meals and dinners.

For this reason, there is a rise in the demand for part-time family chefs. If you love to cook delicious and healthy meals, then this viable business would act as a great supplement for your full-time job.

65. Be a Pet Sitter

Who wouldn't love earning cash to care for a beautiful puppy or fluffy cat? The dominance of unattended pets is another result of busy lives. This has resulted in the creation of job opportunities and business ideas for individuals who have the attention, patience, and time to spare.

You can check out Rover and DogVacay for openings. There are individuals who make more than $1,000 a week taking care of pets.

66. Grooming Pets

If pet-sitting is not enough, you can push your services further and add pet grooming or just start off with it. This requires appropriate training, alongside an operating license based on where you are situated. You will also require equipment for grooming.

As stated by PayScale, pet groomers earn around $17,000 to $40,000 or more. This is a great side hustle if you are able to draw in your clients during weekends.

67. Cleaning Pools

Taking a dive in the pool during the hot weather can be quite entertaining. However, it can be a chore to clean. For this reason, lots of pool owners get the services of others to carry out the cleaning on their behalf. If you require the additional cash, and you have no issues about physical activity, then this can be a profitable side hustle for you which you can do during your spare time.

68. Private Sales and Labeling of Products on Amazon

Categorized as one of the most valuable leaders in tech,

Amazon equally has a huge world market where almost anyone can benefit from the growing ecommerce tide as long as you have the appropriate business idea.

However, similar to everything else that has to do with cash, you need to do a little work to make this money. In this scenario, you have to do lots of researching for generic products such as mugs and key chains which you can link your brand to. You will also have to create an inside sales strategy that will aid you in generating profit from your private label side hustle.

69. Recreational Sports Games Officiator

Do you enjoy sports? If so, this can be a great side hustle for you. Presiding non-professional games that take place at college sports fields and community parks can be an exciting method of turning your passion for outdoor activities into a way to bring in cash. You will be able to do this on the weekends and at night after your full-time job hours.

70. Be a Coach for Sport Teams

If you are a fan of sports, nothing would be more intriguing than playing for your best team. However, earning cash to coach a sports team and remaining close to where the action takes place is the next intriguing thing. Aside from the fact that you will pick up new skills, you will also earn cash from getting your team into the right shape with this side hustle.

The average pay for sports coach as stated by the US Bureau of Labor Statistics is around $30,000 or more. If you are wanting to do this side hustle part-time, you should only expect half of this income.

71. Printing T-Shirts

The business of t-shirt retailing is worth a lot of cash. But what if you want to become involved in the manufacturing aspects of things? The business of printing t-shirts is always translated into a very viable hustle for lots of individuals yearly. However, it can take up much of your spare time, so you need to be sure of what you are getting into before going in. This industry worth billions of dollars is home to numerous part-time entrepreneurs and corporate factories, and you can take a slice of this in your spare time as well.

72. Advertising Vehicles

Yes, it is possible to transform your car into a revenue earner by driving for well-known platforms like Lyft and Uber. However, there are other methods of converting mileage into cash as a smart side hustle.

One method of doing this is by advertising vehicles. This has the potential to make you an income of anywhere from $100 - $500 or more every month. Regardless of the kind of car you drive, the exterior of your vehicle is a great location for running ads.

Go through Carvertise, Wrapify, and other similar platforms to get more information about how to start with this side hustle and how you can link with local advertisers.

73. Window Cleaner

Many home-owners love clean windows, but many of them do not have the time nor the expertise to clean these windows the way they want. The same can equally be said about lots of office managers as well. This increases the demand for window cleaners, making it a great side hustle to venture into especially if you are able to clinch a window cleaning contract for a huge office building. If this is a job you are thinking of getting into, check out this elaborate guide on how to begin a window cleaning business from home

74. Work on Mechanical Turk

Mechanical Turk functions in a similar manner to GigWalk and TaskRabbit. It is a platform online where Amazon amass tasks for people who are willing to do them, and those who are would not mind paying for them.

On this platform, you will be able to get the strangest jobs you can think of. This is made a reality on a parallel online platform that runs on visits, likes, surveys, reads, CPCs, and pins alongside other metrics.

However, it is not advisable to think you would become a millionaire doing this side hustle business. The little sums Mechanical Turk users get rarely turns into anything reasonable even if you use all of your spare time doing this side hustle.

It is an ideal opportunity for individuals who are internationally-based with access to the internet and less cost of living then in the United States.

75. Offering Yard Work Services

A huge portion of small businesses and homeowners have lawns that need tending to. Lots of these people get the services of independent providers of yard work to help them deal with their lawn care issues. To begin and maintain a business in yard work services, you require equipment, training, and an expanding network of clients.

In the United States, a full-time ground keeping and landscaping worker reportedly makes an average wage of about $25,000. However, those who do this as a side hustle mostly during the weekends and evenings can expect to make much lower.

76. Become a Public Speaker

If you have a way with words and speaking, then public speaking can be a great side hustle for you to choose. Lots of artisans, medical practitioners, politicians, and other experts earn additional income by delivering seminars and speeches alongside presentations. Professional motivational speakers earn around $90,000 averagely with only that part of their income.

77. College Counseling

College counselors come in all shapes and sizes. Their core duty is to aid in guiding students through a crucial time in their lives. Counselors typically focus on topics such as career advice, athletics, financial aids, and admissions.

There is a range of institutions in search of part-time counselors which makes it a fantastic side hustle. You can equally begin your practice, and charge a fee of around $20-$100 or more every hour for providing consultative services if you are proficient on the subject.

78. Creating Seasonal Decorations

Halloween, Christmas, Valentine's Day, and Mother's Day are among the range of traditional holidays that work as great reasons to delve into crafting and sales of seasonal decorations. After all, businesses and people pay a decent amount of cash for them.

The overall sales of Christmas trees in the United States alone, in 2014, amounted to over $1 billion. Also, you still have other things to cover such as wreaths, holiday lights, and baskets among others, which would make this a side hustle bring you revenue all-year round.

79. Snowplowing

Holidays are great, but along with winter comes to snow — vast piles of it which hinder traffic. Snow can be entertaining for some time, but someone has to clear it up for us to go on with our lives. You can earn extra cash with this side hustle during your spare time by providing ice-removal services.

80. Sales of Handmade Garments and Clothing

With the increasing popularity of online marketplaces for sales of craft like Etsy, individuals with reasonable artisanal skills like woodworking and sewing always have an accessible market for the sales of their products as a side hustle. If you have always had the desire to design and create clothes by hand, then you can begin to transform those fashion ideas into hand sewn, real garments and earn some cash from this side hustle even in your sleep. Clients from all over the globe check out your Amazon and Etsy stores.

81. Refurbishing of Antiques

The market for antiques is not as famous as it was. However, if you love rare old things and have the skills to bring them back to their prior glory, you will still be able to earn money from this industry.

To begin a business of antique refurbishing part-time, you may need to invest some cash in building a standard workshop and stoking it with all the proper treatments and materials if you want to excel in this side hustle. Begin small by loaning equipment from friends when possible, and learn the fundamentals of the trade as a side hustle before you invest your funds buying lots of equipment.

82. Dance Instructor

Lots of individuals, even those who blatantly deny it, enjoy moving their bodies. It is also a fantastic workout. If at some period of your life, it was necessary to leave your dancing shoes behind for a reasonable office job, nothing stops you from earning cash doing it as a side hustle around your full-time job.

As a part-time dance instructor, you get a part of the amount that full-time counterparts benefit from, but it can translate to a reasonable amount weekly if you are consistent.

83. Bicycle Delivery

It may seem unbelievable, but most freelance bike messengers make more cash than some individuals stuck on an office chair. You may not make millions, but you would certainly make a decent amount of cash. Even Uber is making plans for a delivery service, and organizations like Amazon and WunWun are placing more emphasis on same-day delivery, thus enhancing the demand for more individuals to take advantage of this idea. If you have a great bicycle, then it may be a ticket to earning a decent extra income.

84. Makeup Services

If you have a skill for aiding individuals in looking their best and have an idea of how to captivate using eyeliners and lipsticks, try utilizing your beauty skills to chase this side hustle which you can easily profit from.

For less than $2,000, you can begin your own business as a makeup artist which can be the foundation for a possibly viable business that brings in profit mostly by WOM and referrals from your satisfied customers.

85. Flipping Cars

Flipping cars can be an amazing method of transforming your passion for vehicles into a side hustle. However, you would require capital and the capacity to take risks to be successful in this job. Purchase and sales of cars are just like other Buy low and sell high models of businesses. However, the potential of profit for each hour you invest can be on the high side.

As stated by 3HourFlip.com, the trick is learning how to draw car deals to you, so you will be able to reduce the time you invest and enhance your profit on every sale you make in the side hustle.

86. Marketing Consultant for Small Businesses

If you are experienced with SEO, marketing, or you have experience in getting others excited about services and products you regularly use, consider fine-tuning your skills and utilizing them working as a marketing consultant for small businesses in your area. This is especially the case if you are able to become a local SEO expert and can aid local clients in getting higher ranking in their search results as a side hustle.

Businesses of various sizes constantly have the requirement of bringing in more clients, which is where you can be of help with your side hustle idea.

87. Professional Organizing

If organizing your home is a thing which comes naturally to

you, and you enjoy assisting other individuals, consider a side hustle of being a professional organizer. As the requirement for downsizing grows in various organizations, you can utilize your decluttering and organizing skills to begin making an industry standard of $50-125 each hour with very minimal costs.

Professional organizers are not useful to hoarders alone. Lots and lots of more individuals are beginning to hire professional organizers, so they can stop wasting money and time as a result of the stress that comes from daily disorganization. The best part is that you will be able to do this as a side hustle during the weekends and after work when your customers would equally be at home.

88. Rent Your Space Out

Individuals are always in search of unique venues for weddings, meetings, and parties. Why not make some cash off the space you own already by renting it out for events? If you are the owner of a unique location like a boat, warehouse, or studio, companies like Tagvenue will link you with customers in search of a special location for hosting events.

89. Floral Design

There are numerous occasions all through the year when people will have to order flowers. These could include weddings, birthdays, and Valentine's Day. The best part about this side hustle is that once you familiarize yourself with it, you can keep your costs low if you have a great location to source flowers, and the margins are around 300 percent or above on cut flowers which makes this side hustle a viable one in the appropriate area.

90. Recycling

This is a kind of dirty job which is certainly not for all individuals. Recycling containers of products thrown away can become a really good side income if you put in your best efforts.

Going to events like outdoor concerts and street fairs can be great locations to check out for containers. You would be able to sell off these items on eBay for $4/pound.

91. Removal of Litter for Local Businesses

Similar to recycling, this side hustle needs you to be able to work physically. If you love to work outdoors, then you will be able to make a reasonable amount of side income cleaning up litter outside offices, retail stores, and industrial properties. This is the case especially for organizations with huge parking lots that require frequent cleaning.

Property management organizations require their properties to be litter free, and you will be able to do this using cheap equipment. Charge a fee of $30-$50 per hour and bill your customers the same contact price every month. You can take a look at Clean Lots to find out more on how to begin a litter-removal service.

92. Become a Career Coach

Have you determined how to land jobs with higher pay without hassles? If you have a knack for aiding your co-workers or friends navigate the process of getting the job of their dreams, negotiating a better pay, getting a pay raise in their present job, or nailing an interview, other individuals would be willing to part with cash for your assistance which makes it an ideal side hustle that won't require excess time.

Begin by uploading advice on your blog. You can also become a career coach on platforms with an existing audience of individuals in search of ways to go further in their careers like The Muse. From there, you can emphasize on aiding others to attain actual results, developing case studies to support this side hustle, and finally charging for the outcomes you offer to customers.

93.   *Sales of Life Insurance*

Do you enjoy meeting new individuals? Then, the sales of insurance products, especially life insurance, may be a fantastic way of bringing in some additional cash and growing residual income during your free time.

Selling insurance as a side hustle can rapidly provide you with a stable $500-$2,000 monthly depending on the amount of time you put into it. To begin, you may need to take a course online to improve your knowledge on the topic, and then pass the licensing exam for your state. The biggest issue you will deal with as a new agent is amassing sales past just family and friends.

After that, the remainder would have to be on lead generation and networking to develop this side hustle.

94.   *Editing and Writing Resumes*

Everyone is aware that it can be challenging to locate and land your ideal job. This is mostly the case if you have been stagnant in one position for a long time, and your resume does not seem appealing and fresh.

Before you go on to become a professional resume writer, you will need to learn how to write a resume yourself. Then, you can practice by redoing the resumes of your co-workers and friends. Your next step after this should be to become a part of a resume writers' association, keep proving your credibility, and eventually, you will be able to find your way into more viable opportunities.

95. Become a Part-Time Mover

Perhaps, you don't want a desk job or something online, and you have no hassles physically, then this side hustle is a great choice for you. If you also enjoy working alongside other individuals, then being an on-call mover will suit you. When an individual is moving, they will always require a few helping hands. You can offer this service, and earn some income. Irrespective of if it is assisting someone who is changing apartments or collaborating with a local mover who requires an additional set of hands, a side-gig as a mover can be quite profitable.

There is equally an application that can help you with his business idea; it is known as Bellhops. You will be able to sign up and begin working as a mover instantly after you have gone through the application process. The wonderful aspect of using this app is that they have clients booked and are ready to plan their moves. This means you would have a continuous stream of moving jobs based on where you are situated, just by registering and setting up your available hours.

Chapter 6: Side Hustles for Auto Mechanics

Do you know that as an auto mechanic, working for other people is not the only way to make money? You can make some good money by working for yourself.

If you work as an auto mechanic, there are lots of opportunities for you to make money. Auto mechanics possess specific abilities which a lot of people do not have. As an auto mechanic, you can convert your skills into great ventures for making money. There is no guarantee that it is something you have an interest in. Nonetheless, it is vital that you go through some of the opportunities available to auto mechanics.

Ways for Auto Mechanics to Make Extra Money

Service Cars on the Side

One of the most reliable ways to earn side income as an auto mechanic is to do some jobs on the side. Although a lot of people are not aware, certain folks do not like going to dealerships when the time for servicing comes. If any of these people are aware that you will be able to offer them the right service when they are not in a dealership, they will be willing to pay for it. As a result of this, you can make people in your neighborhood aware that you work as an independent auto mechanic. With this, you will be able to make a lot of money by the side.

You Can Inspect Used Cars

Before going on to purchase a car, a lot of people will be very appreciative if there can be a review of the vehicle they intend to buy. As an auto mechanic, you can be of help to individuals that are searching for a used car to purchase.

As soon as they find a car they love, they will reach out to you. You will then proceed to inspect the vehicle and make sure it is in an excellent working condition before giving them the go-ahead to make the purchase. There are lots of opportunities for auto mechanics that are into the inspection of cars. Amazingly, a lot of these opportunities are still untouched. This is not far from functioning as an independent mechanic. However, unlike an independent mechanic, you will be more into offering services to people that are looking to purchase used cars.

Create Your Own Business

As an auto mechanic, if you are very skilled in the art of fixing damaged cars and making them function like they never had a fault, you can get involved in repairing already abandoned vehicles and putting them up for sale when you are done fixing them. You could make a lot of money if you can put in a lot of time and effort into fixing cars that have packed up. This is because after paying some cash for the vehicle in its terrible state and buying some spare parts, there will be no need to spend any more money. You will be solely responsible for the needed labor and will, therefore, make all the profit alone.

As an auto mechanic, there are lots of unique ways you can make money on the side. However, to explore these many opportunities, you should not put in all your efforts into working for other people. It is essential that you have an open mind and be on the lookout for opportunities. You never can tell when you will find an opportunity that you are interested in.

Chapter 7: Side Hustle for Programmers

There is no denying the fact that software engineers earn pretty high salaries. So, they can live comfortably based on the wage they receive monthly. However, we have some programmers who like to explore other opportunities different from their primary job. They do this to make additional income to complement what they earn monthly.

Are you considering early retirement? Or do you want to gather enough money so that you will be free and won't have to worry about finances or being sacked from your place of work?

There are a lot of reasons why a programmer would want an additional source of income besides the fat salary. These reasons differ from one engineer to another. Here are some side hustles for programmers:

Passive Investment

A lot of programmers like the idea of saving money because it is very easy to do. Once you receive your salary, you can get it deposited into your bank account.

Saving is possible as long as you don't overspend. When you save over a period, your net worth is bound to increase.

One thing you need to know is that depositing money in the bank is not always the best because it slows down the rate at which your net worth grows. The best way to build your wealth is to invest it in something lucrative.

Instead of going for an investment that takes your time, why not focus on passive investing. This involves investing in a company that you consider financially strong and safe. Invest in those companies and watch your portfolio grow with time.

You can make use of the robo-advisors if you don't have the knowledge of the company to invest in. Some of the robo-advisor that you can use is Betterment or Wealthfront.

However, you should not be over ambitious, and don't expect a huge return.

However little the returns might be, it is better than an idle fund in your bank account.

Start Your Programming Blog

If you are not too familiar with stock or you prefer another area of investment, you can earn additional income by kicking off your blog.

What you stand to gain here is that you will not only be amassing wealth, but you will also make yourself relevant in the world of programming.

To open a lot of opportunities in your career, you must know how to sell yourself to people that matter.

The programming blog will be an avenue to teach others about programming and at the same time improve your skills as a programmer. Don't forget you are also making money as you do this, which is great.

Let's pause to think about this – how can a programmer make money from a programming blog?

Well, there are several ways through which you can make money from your blog. Let's take a look at them:

- **Advertisement**

The first way to make money through your blog is to put ads on it.

Google Adsense is an excellent place to start if you don't have any ideas about how to add advertisements to your blog.

Google will authorize you to put Google ads on your website, and you will always get a share of the Ad revenue each time any of your readers clicks on the ad.

An excellent way to increase your income through this means is by looking for ways to increase your readers because your revenue from the ads depends significantly on the number of readers your site can attract.

Once you have gotten used to Adsense, you can start exploring other premium ad agencies.

For instance, coding, horror, and codewars are popular programming sites; they make use of carbon ads.

- **Being an Affiliate**

The second way you can make money through your site is by becoming an affiliate marketer. It involves trying to sell the products of other people through your site.

For instance, you can start selling Amazon Products on your website by signing up with Amazon associate. This is an excellent idea because Amazon has almost everything that is under the sun.

You will be given a referral link when you sign up on Amazon. So, if your readers visit Amazon sites through your referral link and buy anything on those sites, you will be given a commission.

The commission is different, and it is based on factors like your performance, the product, and many other variables.

You should suggest a product that will catch the attention of your readers since they are interested in programming; you should buy products that will be very useful to programmers. Examples of such products are software and books that are based on programming.

Note that you may be asked to recommend expensive products that you have no idea about, and this is very dangerous. So, whatever product you recommend, make sure it is a product you have used personally. This is very important because you must try your best to maintain your integrity and keep the trust and respect your readers have for you. Don't forget, trust is the most valuable link between you and your readers.

Therefore, always make sure you recommend products that are tested and proven to be good. The main point here is that if you don't use a product, never recommend it.

- **Selling Your Own Product**

The third way through which you can monetize your blog is by selling your products. This may require a lot of work on your part, but it is gratifying.

Once you have done your part by setting up the products you want to sell, your blog will take it from there and continue to generate passive income for you.

You must make sure that your product is in line with the interest of your reader.

What you are selling should add value to computer scientists and programmers.

For instance, you can decide to sell books or other products that are related to software engineering careers and programming.

You should note that selling your product may not come easy.

There are lots of things you must learn especially how to market your product effectively and the right way to promote yourself.

So, if you have decided to start selling your product on your website, you have made a great decision, and it is never going to be a waste of time.

Start Your Own YouTube Channel

You can start your personal YouTube Channel if you want to be closer to your audience and you have an endearing personality.

Do you believe that most software engineers could put some of their experience into use when it comes to public speaking?

There are a lot of advantages if you can work on your communication and public speaking skills. So, there is a lot of gains in starting your own YouTube Channel.

Starting a YouTube channel could be better than starting a blog because you will build a better and stronger bond with your audience. The best idea is to have both.

Now, how do you make money on YouTube? Making money on YouTube is not very different from monetizing your blog. Just like blogs, you can make money on YouTube through YouTube ads, selling your products or affiliate links.

Create a Video Course

Another way to make additional money as a programmer is by creating a video course. It is worth noting that there are lots of vacancies for programmers, meaning that programming is in high demand at the moment.

With the increase in demand for programmers, you can make a lot of money through programming as well as teaching others the skill.

Yes, you can make money when you teach programming because there are hundreds of thousands of people in the world who are keen on learning it.

So, if you are skilled in this regard, this could be an excellent opportunity for you.

You can make use of platforms like Udemy to create your courses, and start making money from them. All that is required of you is to create a high-quality course, and they will help you with the marketing and everything else.

Build a Piece of Software and Sell It

This is another way to make additional income, and it requires you to make a piece of software and sell it.

The work of a programmer is to write software. Basically, you can decide to make software and sell it by yourself instead of writing it for someone else to sell.

Programming skills are not the only requisite to achieve this; you need to be knowledgeable about business needs and opportunities.

So, develop software you think will be in high demand or build software that will solve a general problem, and you will make your money.

Your marketing skill is also vital as it will be needed to promote your software.

Unfortunately, an average programmer does not have these marketing skills; it will be a significant advantage if you can learn essential skills as it will be of significant advantage to you.

It is not every programmer that tries to make their software succeed. But, if efforts are made toward making the product succeed, it can be very lucrative.

There are lots of things you can do, and you can develop a phone application, a SAAS service or software that is downloadable.

Publish an eBook on Your Own

Self-publishing a book is a lucrative side hustle idea that a programmer can consider. Self-publishing an eBook is quite easy because there are almost no restrictions to entry. To publish an eBook, register on Leanpub with $99, and you are in.

Learnpub is a self-publishing platform that gives you the opportunity to write an eBook and start selling it. With their robust marketing strategy, your book will be accessible to lots of people right from the first day.

You can also expand your horizon beyond Leanpub as well. They will help you convert your eBook into EPUB, MOBI, and PDF formats, giving you the opportunity to submit your work to other bookstores like Amazon. Comparatively, it is easier to publish an eBook on Amazon.

Benefits of Publishing on eBook

- You find it very easy to recover your initial investment
- Publishing an eBook enables you to establish credibility and authority
- You have a privilege to know more about promotion and product launch

Chapter 8: Side Hustle for Engineers

As far as career options are concerned, engineering can be considered quite a rewarding option. A lot of engineers can comfortably earn between $60,000 and up to six figures per annum. Although the amount that engineers earn is above average, a lot of them are still not comfortable with the amount that they earn. Well, there are quite many reasons for this. Student loans cannot take care of themselves, great vacations have to be paid for, and retirements have to be planned.

Irrespective of the reason you need to make some more money, you might be of the idea that it is not possible. This is even more likely if you are going through classes intended for another degree and working simultaneously. Although it is not impossible to get another job, having a little income just from packaging groceries will not do a lot for you. You are actually in need of a side hustle. A hustle that can help you make good cash on the side and will give you the opportunity to hone your skills and build a stronger profile.

What Can Engineers Do?

In as much as certain side hustles can be handled by virtually everyone (e.g., the sale of tickets and Uber driving), there exists certain side hustles that are perfectly suitable for the skills of an engineer.

Tutoring

It is not a break from the norm for engineering undergraduates to be on the search for engineers that have acquired a lot of experience to assist them in their course of study. There are chances for you to be of help to students in high school science courses, as well as mathematics. This, however, has a lot to do with your background and specialty. You do not have to be with someone in person to be able to tutor them. You can decide to work with people from all parts of the world by signing up to online tutoring services. As an individual that is currently going through their masters, tutoring can be a perfect form of side hustle while you try to make some money with your graduate degree.

Writing

Are you good with words? If so, then writing is one way you can make a good amount of money on the side. All you need to do is work with your skill. A lot of firms are in search of technical writers that can work on projects such as blogs, whitepapers, and instruction manuals. Also, they pay decently for them. If you are able to draft a whitepaper for any engineering company successfully, you could make up to $10,000. With blog posts, you can make some hundreds of dollars. All jobs that have to do with writing can be found on freelance writing job boards. You can also get them through networking. Also, by writing your books, it is possible to create opportunities for yourself. A certain engineer was able to successfully convert his wealth of experience into a series of books for children. He was able to make money from these books by selling them online. There are lots of ways to self-publish your book. You can also decide to work with regular publishers.

Consulting

Consulting is one of the profitable ways to make money by the side. With the right experience and knowledge, it is possible to work with some firms as a consultant. While at this, you can bring your wealth of experience to the table and earn a handsome amount for doing so. You might get involved in projects that are just in their planning phase. There is also a possibility of being a witness in a trial. As far as consulting is concerned, there is one thing that should be avoided. That thing is to ensure that there is no conflict of interest. A conflict of interest could arise if you work with anyone that your employer considers being a rival. It could also mean being a part of a project that your employer has their eyes on.

If you take out some time to brainstorm, you will be able to come up with a lot of other ideas. While at this, it is essential that you can come up with ideas that do not look like work. However, these ideas should be able to help you make some money. Ensure you do not bite more than you can chew, and you will be financially free in no time.

Chapter 9: Side Hustles for Graphic Designers

As a graphics designer, there are a lot of opportunities to make money apart from the regular means of working with a printing and publishing firm, an advertising firm, or freelance jobs. A lot of opportunities exist on the side for good money to be made primarily with the kind of skills you have. These opportunities could be turned into businesses that will make you reach the goals you have financially to be achieved much faster.

But then, good things never come easy. The challenge you would face here is with keeping up your performance levels whilst juggling between your full-time job and making progressive inroads with building your side business.

Below are a few side hustles graphic designers can pick up:

Niche Photography Sales

If you have a passion for taking pictures apart from been a graphics designer, why not turn this passion into a business? You are most likely thinking of delving into the stock photos scenery as soon as you saw photography, but that is an oversaturated scene which is no longer as lucrative as before. The market for stock photos is now so competitive, and it would not serve you best to enter into it.

Your best bet would be to create a niche for yourself in the general photography scene. Look for what interests you - it could be birds, the beach scenery, the green life - and gradually develop your niche photograph collection. There is money to be made from it, as is evident from a Netflix documentary series titled **"Tales by light."**

There are many questions you need to ask yourself though, such as: how can you make your photos unique enough to capture people's attention? Do you need a particular camera lens that captures different angles? Or maybe you need a different means of power photo processing.

Designing T-Shirts for Amazon Merchandise

The t-shirt business is seen by many people as a business with a market that is highly competitive, for the simple reason that it is so easy to enter. But amid this highly competitive business scene, they are individuals who still make lots of good money from it, as high as $10,000 a month!

The t-shirt business is a business model that is easy to enter as they are a lot of companies in this market who have a demand for your skills. However, for your own t-shirt business to stand out from amongst the competition that exists, you must log in a lot of man-hours to steadily make your brand a top-rated choice.

The opportunities in the t-shirts printing business are so vast with various platforms available where your graphics designing skills could be used for your financial gain. It is a great side business as you do not need that huge a capital to kick start it.

One of the best and lucrative platforms out there and which was just launched by the giant American merchandise, Amazon, is the "invite-only" platform: **Merch By Amazon.**

Produce Distinct Poster Designs

If you are very adept at making very colorful, interesting drawings and photos of places you have traveled to, why not open an online shop to sell such items? This would be better than just having them admired by you and your friends.

Selling of Design Templates

If you have the penchant for producing beautiful layouts that can be used by architects or the ordinary layman, there is a huge chance that you will gain a lot financially from the sales of such items. All you have to do is be very creative in your design of such templates. Various platforms give you the space to showcase your design templates such as Creative Market.

The great thing about templates is that they are produced once but can be sold as often as is possible. Producing design templates suited to different tastes increases your financial income while making your brand of templates have a wide reach as well.

You can visit **Creative Markets** to check what templates they have on display.

Sell Customized Maps

Do you love traveling? Do you always list out spots you plan on visiting or those you visited? You can share your best spots by creating an amazing map. Aside from the fact that it is great for you, it would also be great for others.

It is not compulsory that you are a traveler. This idea is also applicable to your immediate environment. You can create maps with places visitors can check out in your hometown or locations to eat. Maps are ideal methods of decorating the inner parts of your home and always get the attention of individuals. You will also be able to earn a decent amount of cash.

Design Your Own Travel Journal

More people are starting to take more trips around the globe as the world as a whole is getting more easily connected with the advent of modern technologies. First-time travelers and tourists have the desire to make their first experience a memorable one.

If you have traveled to a lot of places around the world, why not take up the idea of creating a travel journal that shows the beautiful places you have been to? Just create a travel journal that deals with a specific niche, make it appealing to interest the pique of people, and make your money.

Even with the advent of modern day travel agents, people still like to have personal knowledge sourced from elsewhere other than these agents.

Decals Designing for Smartphones/Macbooks.

Smartphones, tablets, and MacBooks are the most personal objects people possess nowadays. They have become a part of our everyday lives with people not only wanting to have the best devices but also customize their screens to their taste. They want their devices to portray their personality.

Decal designing is a way of getting started in this side hustle. It is cheap and very fast. You will probably not make a lot of money when you start, but it is still a thing of joy and pride to know that you are making side money effortlessly even while you sleep. To even get further reach easily and make more gains financially, you can create a **domain in this field**.

Society6 and **Etsy** are great platforms through which you can get started with this business.

Have an Online Course

A sweet way of making good money on the side is by having a course online. With your skills as a graphics designer, some people are also willing and eager to acquire such skills as well. Why not use the opportunity to create an online course to share your knowledge and experience?

Creating an online course does require a lot of effort besides research to be carried out, typing, and uploading of educational contents. With dedication and passion, you can create an excellent means of making cool financial incomes.

Skillshare and **Udemy** are websites through which you can have your online course uploaded, and get paid for it.

Become an Infopreneur

This has some similarity with creating a course online, but this requires less effort compared to the online course gig.

You can produce an educational guide or e-textbook making use of the PDF format paired with other Microsoft formats. People will have to buy such a guide online and download to print.

This is a much faster route of having your knowledge imparted to lots of people compared to making a video on a YouTube channel.

Selling Your Design Assets

You would most likely have a design tool that you favor above others as a graphic designer and become a guru with its usage, customizing it to your taste, and having that unique touch of yours. It has now become your design asset.

If you think it could be of benefit to others in the field, why not make a market out of it? It could be customized fonts, icons, bullet heads, plugins, and so on.

Sell EBooks With the Help of Kindle Publishing

As a specialist in the graphics designing field, you can go about writing a book and have it published. In this modern era, it has become easy to have it published with little money as an investment. In comes <u>Kindle Publishing</u>.

Kindle publishing has done a lot in helping book writers as they no longer have to go through the olden day's rigorous route of seeking a publisher. Today, all you have to do is write and upload to Amazon. You make use of the vast global reach Amazon has, and Amazon takes a certain percentage off sales of your eBook.

You can have your financial income from your published books diversified by having a hardcover version, which you can get by using the platform **CreateSpace**.

Selling of Your Home Designs

As a graphic designer, if you enjoy the creation of designs for houses, why not try selling home designs that you created?

There are people who need it so that they can save cost and time. Cost in terms of having to acquire the services of an architect. In terms of time, some people are very much into looking at ready-made house designs.

This field is relatively new, and by nature conservative, it is a great way to push architects into becoming more creative and innovative in their drawings.

Produce Illustrations for Publishers

Looking at the number of articles now written, and which get to be published daily, you cannot help but notice the trend of them being more enlightening in terms of their detailed illustrations, which adds to the articles becoming more complex and sophisticated.

Images and drawings have become more important in conveying messages and support stories told.

Illustration gurus tap into this opportunity by making use of their skills to supply illustrations to publishers, which they would use for their articles.

You can use **Shopify** as an ecommerce shop to display your drawings to a broader horizon. Shopify has a monthly subscription fee, but it does save you a lot of time and provides some helpful web plugins in the marketing of digital products.

Selling Your Works of Art

If you are an artist or have an artistic flair with a particular style that's unique, why not sell your artwork? Why display your artwork at home for people to admire when you can readily make money from selling them?

The domain, **DesignByHumans** is a great platform to sell your works of art.

Selling App Design Templates

We are in an era where to get more market for your business, you must have an application, also known as an app for short in modern lingo. Creating an App takes a lot of time and a considerable investment financially at the start. But this financial investment is a significant burden for small, new startups as they cannot engage the services of skilled software and mobile App developers. Their first motive is to make money to sustain the business.

You can come in by designing ready-made templates through which they can choose any and launch their App easily, with you making the money they would have used to hire skilled App developers.

You can sell your Android or iOS templates on platforms like **MyAppTemplates, AppDesignVault.**

Become a Freelancer

Deciding to start a freelance business is one of the best career decisions you can ever make. Aside from the obvious financial benefits you gain from taking your skills out to the streets for hire at significantly a higher monetary profit compared to your day job, freelancing helps in building and cementing relationships with high-growth startups in your area of specialty. It also helps in giving you a sense of direction as you create a brand of yourself and achieve the future business goals you have for your business.

Build a Membership Community

Designer Hangout, a UX designer platform prides itself to be the first group on Slack having more than 6,000 designers who meet on the platform to discuss everything about designing and user experience(UX). An option for you could be to charge fees for membership as they join your community on Slack, Facebook, or any other popular social media platforms.

Designer Hangout decided to take a different route to make money on their platform. They engage in vetting new requests for membership, and instead of charging fees, they make their money with the partnership they have with companies like Adobe, their regular <u>event series</u>, and their <u>job board</u> listings.

Teach at General Assembly

In the world of design education, <u>General Assembly</u> is a big name. They are frequently on the lookout for skilled experts in this field to hire them for classes they have in 15 major cities of the world and via their online school's system. Their classes offer a wide range of designing topics ranging from basic designing principles, user experience(UX), web designing, and others. An instructor with this educational platform can make a lot of money depending on the number of classes he can handle on a weekly or monthly basis.

Become a Coach Online

Easy-to-use online tools and marketplaces such as <u>Coach.me</u> and <u>Savvy</u> have made the advent of online life and career coaching a lucrative business. The platform is provided to leverage your acquired skills and expertise in ways that give back to society and has been a source of help to others in making meaningful progressive steps in their chosen careers. Becoming a coach online coach is easily a highly-rewarding side hustle. Most coaches online bill either on an hourly basis or per session, offering packages that are topic-based which help their clients accomplish specific goal or goals by the end of the engagement.

Launching a Podcast

Podcasts have become so popular nowadays with the advent of smartphones and tablets. The <u>Despreneur Podcast</u> has created a niche for itself in this industry. Once you can give out podcast content that is of value and attracts people to listen in, you can generate a lot of money. Household brands and a lot of other products will want to sponsor your podcasts once they take a view of the demographics of the audience that tunes in to listen to your podcasts. Endeavor to make your podcasts one of the top-rated podcasts, and you could be on your way to making huge favor monetary gains.

Produce Colorful Physical Products

Designers have a big advantage when it comes to creatively design physical products that can attract people's eyes with their aesthetic value. If you have a talent for producing beautiful illustrations, a side hustle such as a greeting card designer would be an excellent choice for you. You can begin by submitting your designs to sites like Ohhdear and have them tuned into colorful greeting cards without you being personally involved.

You can print your own small cards eventually and make higher financial gains by selling your cards directly to consumers on Etsy.

Chapter 10: Side Hustles for Teachers

Although teaching is a noble profession, it is not a well-paying one. The impact of teachers in the lives of so many can never be overlooked. They are always there to inspire us, encourage us to learn, make meaning out of lives, and even love us like their own kids. A good number of people will not be where they are today without the help of their teachers.

Unfortunately, teachers are underpaid even though they are burdened with the responsibility of lots of students. Hence it is necessary to find a side hustle that complements their job and brings in extra cash.

Though there are lots of side hustles out there that one can venture into. Below is a list of the more suitable for teachers and educators as they are in line with your profession.

Freelance Writing

You can capitalize on your writing skills to earn extra cash for yourself. There are lots of websites and companies out there ready to work with you.

You might want to try out Contena, which is a platform where writing jobs on the web are collated into one large job board. This makes it a lot easier to find writing gigs suitable for you. You can earn as much as $50 to $1000 per article on Contena or any other writing platform. The best part of it is you get to work remotely.

Teaching English Online

Since English is a universal language and a skill on its own, there are lots of people out there who are willing to pay just to learn to speak English. VIPkid is an online platform where Chinese children get to learn to learn English through the help of English-speaking teachers via teleconferencing sessions. As stated on their website, you can earn as much as $22 an hour. The only requirements if you work in Canada or the US are a one-year educational experience and a bachelor's degree. The educational experience is not limited to tutoring; teaching and coaching are also accepted.

<u>VIPkid</u> has made it so easy that you work when it's convenient for you and the difference in time zones makes it even better because it could fit in perfectly into your free hours. Teaching sessions are mostly in the early hours of the day Eastern Time.

The good thing is you do not have to step an inch out your home to do this. All you need to do is apply.

Success Tips After Applying

Immediately after you complete your application, do not forget to schedule a convenient time for your video interview. This process is the most important part of your application.

You will have a live video interview with one of the VIPkid teaching team members, but before that, you will be expected to choose a convenient time for the interview. Have in mind that the team is made up of majorly non-native English speakers, and they are very friendly people. The live interview comes up usually a few days or a week after completing the application.

Driving for Money

Perhaps you've heard of Uber or Lyft. You could sign up with them as a driver. What most people do not know about these platforms is that they have a "Destination Mode" feature. This feature allows you to connect with riders heading your direction daily. How cool is that?

What this means is you sign up with Uber or Lyft, and turn on your app during your free hours to earn some extra cash. Lyft drivers are said to earn $14-17 an hour. You also get to keep all the tips you receive. After your first 100 rides with Lyft, you get a bonus of $250.

Babysitting, Caregiving, and Child Care

You can earn extra cash during the holidays through child care, babysitting, or looking after aged people. This is a good source of income for both teachers and students.

Sites such as Care.com or sittercity.com can help you find people in need of your services. Simply create a free account with them, and you will be connected with potential clients. They have flexible working hours at an hourly rate of $12-15.

If you love sitting around elderly one, you consider caregiving as a side hustle during your free time. You never can tell what would come out of it.

Tutoring

Tutoring is yet another good side hustle option you might want to consider since you love teaching. As a matter of fact, according to reports a Side Hustle Nation reader, it earns $1000 weekly through his part-time tutoring business that preps people for the ACT.

Wyzant is also another useful online platform where you can

create an account, and get connected with students in need of your services. The rating depends on the tutor, subject, and his location although the rates range from $30 to $60 an hour. They have flexible working hours which is most likely after school hours.

Teaching Online

Although direct tutoring is quite lucrative, you are still trading hours for money. The best way to even earn more is to sell your knowledge as an online course on platforms such as Udemy. This is a leading education platform with courses on just about any topic you can think of and millions of students ready to learn. Some people can earn about $4,000-5,000 per month just for teaching simple courses such as how to bake the perfect sourdough bread.

This site is mainly for professional adult courses, which means your normal class curriculum will need some adjustments to fit perfectly into this site. This is an excellent source of additional income as a teacher.

Reselling Your Curriculum

Sites such as Educents and TeacherspayTeachers has made it possible to sell various kinds of educational materials such as lesson plans or curriculum. With these online platforms, you get to share your work with others and get paid for it.

Just like Udemy, your income depends entirely on the number of people that purchase your products, but it's also a good side hustle since it does not affect your working hours.

Online Surveys

Online surveys are another avenue to earn some extra cash during your free time. Although the online survey market has been flooded with different scam sites, there are still genuine ones out there that pay you for your survey even though the pay might be low.

The rate for online survey ranges from $0.5 to $5 per survey, and this can amount to something substantial when done consistently. You also get to do this just about anytime and anywhere.

Airbnb

You can become an Airbnb host if you have an extra room in your apartment to spare. This can be an exciting side hustle, especially during summer break. You get to meet people from different parts of the world, have fun, and get paid for it.

You have full control over the process as you get to set the house rules, availability, and pricing by yourself. Even better, for every rental, there is a $1 million liability insurance attached to it. You can go through their homepage to have an idea of how much you can charge for rental.

Focus Groups

This is an excellent way to rake in some extra cash, and the good thing is that focus groups pay higher than an online survey. You get paid merely for giving honest feedback over a product before it is released to the market.

Initially, focus groups organize guided discussions with participants in a specific location. But with advanced technology, today, focus groups run online where you are only required you to sit in front of a computer and have a video conference with other participants.

Sites such as Respondents.io helps you find opportunities like this where you can earn up to $100 per hour and even more within a month.

Become an Adjunct Professor

You might want to look into becoming an adjunct professor locally or online at any college of your choice if you wish to earn extra cash.

Some technical schools and colleges accept a bachelor's degree and working experience although the common requirement is a master's degree. The interesting thing about this is a lot of adjunct professor gigs allows you to record your lectures and use them repeatedly.

On average, adjunct professors earn $2,200 to $3,500 per course, and the working hours are very flexible.

Self-Publishing

You could earn some extra cash by publishing your books if you enjoy writing. Amazon helps you sell your books directly to the market without the need of a publishing company.

Become a Coach

If you've got great dancing skills or are good at sports, you can earn some money from becoming a coach. There are lots of dance studios and gyms in your surroundings in need of skilled coaches. There could even be an opening for you at the school where you teach. As a youth soccer coach, you can earn about $18 to $25 an hour while a dance instructor earns $20 an hour. This is a good way to earn extra money just by doing what you love doing.

Voiceover Work

As a teacher who is used to constant talking, you can earn some more cash as a voiceover actor. If you've got an acting skill and a unique voice to compliment it, you could work as a voiceover actor, and get paid for it.

On average, the pay of a voiceover actor ranges from $100 for a 15-second recording to as high as $3000 for an audiobook. Platforms such as ACX.com or Voices.com can help find beautiful opportunities like this. You can also work from home if you have the necessary equipment or in a good studio. Most importantly, you get to work at a convenient time for you.

Chapter 11: Side Hustles for Drivers

In today's world, the business industry is no longer dominated by white-collar jobs. Businesses created by bright minds to solve the needs of society without being confined within the strict definition of a collar job. Several rewarding job opportunities are considered profitable and financially satisfactory. One of these businesses involves driving for a living. There are several ways you can make a living through driving:

Truck driving

Operating a truck is considered one of the most common driving jobs. It is also known to be one of the steady jobs due to the tremendous shortage of qualified drivers, and as a result, different companies are now paying their drivers extra for signing and also for licensing fees. Looking at the stated statistics, truck driving can be considered a great job opportunity. Truck driving cannot be outsourced since consumers purchase various kinds of commodities frequently. Consequently, there will always be a need for drivers to transport these commodities to them.

Recently, truck driving jobs have been reported by Reuters to increase to 35,000, and they will increase more in a few years to come. This goes further to show the accessibility and flexibility of the job to interested candidates. However, if this description does not fit your preference, there is another type of truck driving job known as a tow truck driver. A tow truck driver's job description is the hauling of cars with mechanical problems or vehicles involved in accidents. A tow truck driver can also act as a repossession agent. It should, however, be noted that the earning of a tow driver is largely dependent on his employment status, that is whether he/she is an employee or he/she is the owner of the business. As an employee, his income is solely dependent on how accurately he markets his services than on his ability to drive.

Pet Taxi Service

According to an old proverb - A business person is all about solving problems. There are a lot of people who own pets and find it difficult to visit the vet because of lack of transportation or their busy schedule. Pet taxi services are about driving animals on a round trip to their vet. This type of driving job presents a good opportunity to make a decent living. For instance, companies like Pet Taxi Service can bill the sum of $100 to $200 per trip. This kind of rate is, however, different in other cities, but one can make an honest living if you choose to engage in pet taxi services.

Driving a School Bus

This type of job is suitable for people who desire to drive a bus and still have a sufficient amount of time to do other things. The job is known to be flexible, and as such, the driver can work part-time and only during the school year. According to the Bureau Labor Statistic (BLS) report, the minimum annual wages of a school bus driver are $28,330. To fit perfectly well into the category of a school bus driver, you must have the following traits: a) you must be an early riser, b) you must love working with children, and c) you must be very patient in the job.

Shuttle Driver

Another job available to you as a driver is driving a shuttle. The job description of a shuttle driver entails transporting people to and fro a specific location on a bus or a van. These vans or buses come in various sizes, and it could be an oversized van, a regular bus, or a small-sized electric vehicle. Shuttle driver activities are usually confined within a specific route and distance as determined by the employer. A classic example is when a shuttle driver's route is restricted to hotels and airports or parking lots. An apparent setback for this kind of job is that the shuttle driver's activities are on repetition, such that he engages in the same routine daily. This, however, makes the job safe and predictable.

Chauffeur

According to a report made by the Bureau of Labors, chauffeurs and taxi drivers both earn a median wage of $22,840 per annum. This, however, is considered false, as chauffeurs are usually tipped by their passengers but unlikely to report such addition to their employers. Consequently, a chauffeur's wage might be higher than what is reported. According to indeed.com, the reported minimum wage of a chauffeur is $28,000, presumably excluding tips, if any.

Taxi Driver

Taxi driver jobs are one of the most popular jobs in the driving sector. Especially in recent times, where the likes of Uber, licensed hackney cabs, and taxi companies are in full operation. A taxi driver is bound to make more in an urban area than a rural area, but this is not a setback as you can take a nap for some time before setting out again. The Bureau Labor Statistics stated that taxi drivers earn a median of $22,840 annually, excluding tips from customers, as they are unlikely to report the tips.

Delivery Drivers

One of the duties of a delivery driver is ensuring timely delivery of goods. These goods are primarily the products of the companies you work for. For instance – Domino's pizza delivery driver has the responsibility to deliver orders made by customers to a particular route. If you are exceptional in providing timely delivery, some customers will tip graciously. The official statistics on how much a person who delivers pizza makes can be considered false, as employees are most likely to underreport the tips they get. One of the advantages of working as a pizza delivery driver is that you shuffle between jobs or work only on weekends.

Another kind of delivery driver is those that deliver newspapers. Some drivers deliver newspapers to individuals' homes while others operate a location filling coin-operated boxes, thus distributing bundles of newspaper to carriers who then deliver on foot or by bicycles. These drivers are mostly hired as independent contractors and have no benefits aside from the fixed rate for a location or per paper. If you search the website called www.indeed.com for newspaper delivery, over 2,000 jobs or more come up. According to the site, a person can earn the sum of $850 to $1200 per month. This job can be done side by side other shifts, as it is considered flexible and takes only a few hours of your day.

Driving a City Bus

If you are looking out to make good cash, driving a city bus might be the best way to go, especially if you are willing to work unconventional hours. According to the report made by the Wisconsin State Journal, a city bus driver who puts in hours can make over $159,258 per annum. This is possible if you are in a large city. The BLS report also stated that the median annual wage for inter-city bus drivers is $38,750 for some while others make up to $48,510 or more.

Other Driving Jobs

The above listed are not the only type of driving jobs available, you can also search on various websites for driving jobs like indeed.com, monster.com, careerbuilder.com, simplyhired.com, snagajob.com

When searching, simply use words like a chauffeur, driving, or delivery. You will find interesting or not so interesting jobs, such as furniture delivery driver, chauffeur, pizza delivery driver, or truck driver. It is your duty to pick which one fits you best. Also, note that you can get paid to drive your own car by signing an agreement with ridesharing services. Please be aware that this is not a regular job.

Be Your Own Boss

If you own a pick-up truck, here are some side hustles you can begin on your own, they include:

Hauling

There are people in your immediate community or beyond who need to haul away some of their items, but they do not own a pick-up truck or have access to one. You can start your business with your pick-up truck by rendering your services to them. For example, some people who work as yard caretakers may need to haul equipment around. You can offer your services by loading into your truck some of their stuff such as lawnmowers, trimmers, rakes, or other equipment to their desired destination. You can also advertise this business in your local newspaper or tell people what you now do. If you don't know how much to charge, ask the local stores around you, and charge less than the original prices. This is not to put your new business out, but this is to draw in customers.

Moving

Another idea is charging for moving items from one place to another with your pick-up truck. Observe how you can be of help to others, and at the same time try and make a little profit. When the people observe that your services go beyond simply renting a truck, it will prompt them to hire you, as it is an advantage to them, even if it might cost them more than usual. Start by building your clientele.

Before you start your pick-up truck hustle, make sure you find out all the requirements needed to smoothly operate your kinds of business, such as business license requirements or insurance requirements. Also, take into cognizance tax deductible against your business income.

Chapter 12: Side Jobs for Law Enforcement Officers

In contradiction to some people's opinion that the work of a law enforcement officer is easy, their job is known to be stressful, dangerous, and takes a toll on their personal lives generally. This does not take away the fact that the job is satisfactory and equally rewarding. Due to the nature of a law enforcement officer's job, the possibility of a side-job is not generally considered.

Below are a few ways in which a law enforcement officer can generate more income or provide other means in which they can serve humanity and still keep their job.

Volunteer Firefighter

To volunteer means to engage one's services without monetary consideration in exchange. This type of side job is perfect for a law enforcement officer who desires to render the public his services through firefighting. Due to a law enforcement officer's training and skills, they can protect their community, and such an act is highly commendable, noticed, and appreciated. It goes further to create a platform for learning new skills and an opportunity to stay in shape continually.

Private Investigator

As water and oil do not mix well, it is common knowledge that a law enforcement officer and a private investigator do not, for the most part, share a cordial relationship. A law enforcement officer's ability to work as an independent contractor as a private investigator will serve as an added advantage to potential clients, the reason being that a law enforcement officer can easily identify boundaries and display extra caution. The nature of a private investigator's job will serve as a great side job opportunity as it brings in good cash.

Restaurant/Café Owner

There are instances where a law enforcement officer has made enough money through the stock market, or through inheritance, it is then a great idea to purchase a restaurant or a café with the money. One cannot overemphasize the advantage of having more than one stream of income. It might sound impossible to work as a law enforcement officer and at the same time own a restaurant of your own, but this is possible as the administration of the business will be the primary function of an employee, while you make the crucial decisions regarding the company. This type of side job is not readily available to everyone but those who have money and can spare sufficient time.

Blogging

As a law enforcement officer, it is inevitable not to witness entrancing stories in your field. These stories can serve as materials for a blog, and as such, you can earn money by starting a blog and sharing stories from the perspective of a law enforcement officer. Note that this type of business is only deemed profitable after some time, then your blog can be used for advertisements and sponsorship.

Photography

This is a job criterion for a law enforcement officer to have keen observation skills. This skill can be channeled into a money-making business as a photographer. An exceptional photographer is one who captures the true nature of anything remarkable. These pictures can be sold to different websites and blogs for the right amount of money, as these platforms are known to buy stock images for a considerably great price.

Lawn Care

If you are in search of a therapeutic and lucrative side job as a law enforcement officer, you should consider working as a lawn caretaker. This job creates an atmosphere that calms your mind, and, at the same time, gives you the opportunity to work outdoors. To get started, all you need to do is inform the people within your community and let them know you are available to mow their lawns for an affordable price. Lawn care as a side job generates a steady flow of income, as this can be repeated for weeks.

Security Planning

Nothing feels better than getting extra money for what you know how to do best. This is the case of security planning for a law enforcement officer, who can serve as a security consultant for event planners, whether it is for a party, a concert, or a community gathering. A law enforcement officer can use his knowledge to manage the security of any given event smoothly. For starters, send out words to your community and inform them about your expertise in providing a safe environment for their events. Once they are aware you are a law enforcement officer, they will be fast to contact you, and as such you will be making a great deal of money.

Chapter 13: Side Hustles for Lawyers

The ethical code for lawyers is sensitive to the extent that it sometimes prevents lawyers from juggling between jobs. For instance, ABA Journal reported the case of Mr. Matthew Scott, a lawyer practicing at the Commonwealth of Kentucky, who was fined by the ethical counsels with the sum of $2,000 for answering questions on a website during his off time at his job.

He did this to earn extra income. This, however, can be prevented if as a lawyer, you are rightly informed on the type of jobs you can engage in without breaching the profession's ethics codes and rules. You can engage in the following activities:

Teaching

A practicing attorney can act as a legal researcher and a writing instructor in a law school. This can serve as a perfect side job as it is acceptable in the legal profession. To start, you are advised to approach the career officer in your local law school to see if there are openings available. You can also consider the opportunity of teaching a law-related course at a college close to you or in an unaccredited law school.

Tutoring

Bar exams and the LSAT are known to be must-pass exams for law students and others. This, therefore, serves as a lucrative side job for lawyers who also consider themselves tutors. Also, it should be known that companies who deal majorly on the preparation of private tests such as SAT or ACT are ready to hire lawyers with tutoring skills. This side job is considered lucrative and flexible as your day job is not affected.

Writing and Editing

Lawyers are well-known for their writing skills and excellent grammar. This skill can be employed by bloggers or website owners who are in dire need of good writers and editors, to either edit their publication or write an eBook. This is a perfect side job for legal practitioners attached to a small law firm or for those who practice alone.

Hosting a Legal Call-In Show

Lawyers, in general, are allowed to share their knowledge of the law on televisions or radios. This, however, does not generate a direct income but serve as publicity or advertisement to potential clients, who will then seek out your law firm, for consultancy or engagement of a brief.

ADR/Mediation

Alternative dispute resolution (ADR) is open to both lawyers and judges. It becomes a perfect side job, where the former is skilled in negotiation and can serve as a neutral arbitrator in various cases or dispute. If you are a lawyer that has practiced for at least 10 years, you can also consider becoming a temporary or small-claims judge. This will secure another means of income for you.

Sports Referee

Lawyers are trusted to rightly differentiate between right and wrong as well as resolve quarrelsome issues between parties where there is a need to. For instance, the man called Ed Hochuli, who happens to be a trial lawyer within the jurisdiction of Phoenix is known as the NFL's most recognized referee. This sounds like an exciting way of making extra bucks if you are into sport.

Consulting for Hollywood

Lawyers are opportune to hear exciting confidential stories of their clients. This is the reason why movies and television series with legal themes consult lawyers for inspirations. You can go further as a lawyer to sell stories that are particularly dramatic to scriptwriters. These stories should not be tied personally to any of your clients, and, as such, do not breach the rule of confidentiality. It can be assured that the payment for this side job is promising.

Temp Counsel

It is common practice in law firms that an external attorney is hired to handle excesses cases that are too much for the firm to do by itself. This is also done in situations where the law firm briefed does not specialize in a particular area of law, and as such, the brief is contracted to another law firm or jointly handled by both law firms. This serves as a good side job as it generates income from another source.

Cases Per Diem

This is known as one of the simplest ways to earn an extra buck as a lawyer. Oftentimes, law firms need lawyers to make an emergency appearance for them in court. This is done majorly for a simple court sitting, such as an adjournment. This is most profitable when it is within your jurisdiction and if you also have a case in the same court on that same date.

Legal Research and Writing

Some lawyers are more skilled at researching and writing than others. If you are one, it is a perfect way to make money as some lawyers will pay a reasonable sum for you to write their briefs and motions. This can be done without affecting your primary duty at your workplace and, as such, serves as a great side job to earn extra income.

Create Your Legal Courses

You can create legal courses designed to teach others a particular subject matter. After drafting and perfectively concluding the work, you will begin to earn money passively, without actively getting involved in teaching. For instance, a criminal attorney can create a legal course called, "secrets to winning cases," and earn from it.

Develop an App

Technology has formed a considerable part of every industry; this can be the same for law. If you have a unique idea of a helpful app, for instance, a calendar app for lawyers to keep track of their cases in court, you can approach a developer, and later on, sell it to websites such as Google and make cool cash from your sale.

eBook Publication

As a lawyer, you can publish an eBook on different things expressing your genius opinion. There are various platforms you can sell it to and make good cash without disrupting your main job as a lawyer.

Create a Podcast

The advantage of creating your podcast, especially if it becomes popular is that you can earn through advertisements and sponsorship. This, however, requires patience and consistently been able to build something worthwhile.

Become a Speaker

Most lawyers are great speakers as it comes with the job description. A lawyer is expected to have an orator's skill and as such make a great speaker. Your popularity as a speaker must be built over time, but once your reputation is out there, you will be able to generate income through this medium. Different organizations will invite you to speak, and pay you for your time.

Write Freelance Articles

The one sure way to earn extra money as a lawyer is writing articles as a freelancer. You must, however, be a good writer to get jobs from blogs or websites. This is done for a reasonable fee and does not have to disrupt your job as a lawyer.

Chapter 14: Side Hustles for Skilled Photographers

There comes a point in the life for every lover of photography when they begin to consider the option of making money off their passion. It could be challenging for someone with a full-time job that is unrelated to photography. However, with careful research, you can figure out a way to earn some extra cash through photography rather than always spending on it.

It could be tough to create a balance between your relationship with friends and family and your time while working a full-time job. Hence it is necessary to find a way to manage your time efficiently. Depending on your skill set, schedule, and interest, some side income options might be more preferable than others. Therefore, it's up to you to make your choice. Having said this, below are a list of options through which you can earn extra cash from photography.

Taking Engagement Photos

Before a wedding takes place, first of all, there needs to be an engagement between the intending couple and a party to celebrate their engagement if they so decide. Who wouldn't want to take beautiful photos on their special day? A lot of wedding photographers combine engagement shoot with wedding shoot as a single package, but people who have no interest to engage in wedding shoot could use engagement shoot as an avenue to venture into the wedding industry. You could partner with an established photographer who does only wedding shoot and offers your engagement shoot services. This will give you the opportunity to gain more visibility and experience.

Weddings

A wedding is a good source of money depending on the services you render. If you can do an amazing wedding shoot, you make the couple pleased with your services and can be recommended. The income from just a few wedding shoots a year is enough to take care of major expenses. You do not necessarily need to have a piece of lighting equipment to get started, simply limit your wedding shoots to outdoor events that take place during the day, so you do not have to worry about lighting equipment.

Family Portraits

A family portrait well-done could be hanging on the wall in someone's home for years to come. A family portrait is also a good source of side income for a photographer, and you can as well get more clients through recommendations. This is lucrative and a fun thing to do as you get to meet and interact with people from different walks of life consistently.

Senior Portraits

Another good source of side income for photographers is taking senior portraits, and this requires less budget, unlike weddings. With the advancement in technology today and the power of social media, your services could be promoted via free social media marketing amongst friends. If you need help or tips on how to publicize your services to the community to begin making money, you can read up Stanley Harper's recent article.

Real Estate

Many photographers do not consider real estate photos as a source of income. This is probably because most real estate agents are impatient and want immediate transformations of the photos which might not be feasible due to the tight schedule of the photographer. If you can figure out a way to make it happen, you can earn some cool amount of money from real estate photos as a side income. Environment sometimes determines the quality of real estate photos. At a certain time in Boston, the real estate market was nothing to talk about as one could easily sell a home with poor cell phone photos. But in an advanced environment where buyers desire to see captivating images, you could make tons of money from real estate photography. It could also open more doors of opportunities for you.

Corporate Headshots

The physical appearance of a company's employees influences the impression the company makes. Good looking employees gives a good impression of their company and vice versa. A company's website can tell whether or not they need new corporate headshots. Make a list of the companies around you and go through their business website, then get in touch with the ones you think might need improved corporate headshots.

Event

The nature of an event determines how often the services of a photographer are needed. So, find the ones that are well-paying or the ones that could bring you profitable opportunities directly. For instance, you can decide to cover an event where the attendees would wish to take personal pictures of themselves and pay for it. You could also choose to shoot an event where you get to meet people who will be willing to work or partner with you in the nearest future.

Product Photography

The good thing about product photography is that it can be done at just about any time. This means it can conveniently fit into your schedule. Place and time is never really a challenge for product photography. Therefore, if you have a regular day job, you can do your shoots at night or over the weekend to reduce the workload, and save yourself some stress. Search for products from local businesses in your community or online retail stores like Amazon and takes photos of them during your free time.

Sport Events

There are different kinds of opportunities that come along with sporting events for a photographer. The specific sport determines your opportunities though. You could get a contract from a newspaper company that wants to cover the event. Friends and families of the participants might also want photos of the events. Sponsors of a team are also potential clients. Even the sport participants themselves could as well want photos of their performance. Most high school sports events work in hand with local newspapers for event coverage but also give room for pictures of participants to be sold to families that wish to have them.

Aside from football and basketball which are the most popular sporting events, shooting other kinds of sports can also serve as a good source of income. Although it's great to get to shoot the lead athletes, you should also pay attention to others associated with the event such as the band members, cheerleaders, and color guards. To create better opportunities for yourself, you might want to look into sports that are less appreciated and make great photos of them.

Sell Prints

Knowing the right environment where your prints get seen the most can give you the opportunity to sell them for good cash. A quaint bakery might be a good place where people go to relax, but it's never a good place to display a portrait. Try to avoid situations where people only go to spend little or no money, such as at banks, libraries, and pastry shops. There are two great places where you can get the most out of your photo display. They are tourist attractions and bars.

Gift shops, breweries, craft fairs, wineries, and art galleries are great places where you can sell your prints. This is because sites like these are visited by potential buyers who are willing to spend money on quality items. It is even better to choose places where you get to pay little commission unless the places that charge higher can get you something much better.

If you would prefer to sell from home rather than in person, you can create a personal online store on Fine Art America, Etsy, or even on your own website.

Never relent at promoting your prints. Offer discounts and coupons regularly to encourage your customers and motivate them to keep buying. Figure out other strategies that will help you reach out to more people daily.

Stock Photography

Since it is now very common to make money off a landscape photo shoot, you could try to explore other niches with less attention. In the world we live in today, photos are required to promote almost every industry. Think about any aspect of life that is poorly represented with pictures and create an opportunity for yourself off it.

Teaching

If you've become well familiarized with your camera to the point where you can earn money off it, you might want to consider teaching since you are knowledgeable in that area. If you lack the confidence to face a large group of people, then you can organize a one on one class with your students. If you have a tight schedule and can't make out time to shoot, you can teach your students via Skype or any other convenient online platform. Since cameras are now very much affordable, no student who desires to gain knowledge on the usage of a camera won't be left behind.

Lead Workshops

Workshops are quite different from teaching because there are different sections involved. Being a workshop leader, you need to be hospitable and ensure that your attendees are having a nice time. You are indirectly playing the role of a tour guide. The workshop requires more work such as getting a permit or insurance that you previously do not have, and a lot of planning is involved. This could be a good source of side income if it is done well.

Food Photography

There are lots of restaurants out there in need of a photographer to capture their meals. Food photography does not require so many equipment; basic ones will do. Go through the websites of various restaurants within your environment just as with corporate headshots, and reach out to those you think might need your services as a food photographer.

Write for a Photography Website

You could write an article for a photography website and make money off it. If you are knowledgeable in photography and love writing at the same time, writing photography-related articles for websites could be a great way to make money off your passion. Find sites in need of your materials, and sell them to interested buyers at a fair price.

Drone Photography

Opportunities are all around us. It all depends on how we utilize them. Since the introduction of drones some years ago, more opportunities that would help people earn extra cash through photography have been created. For places that cannot be easily accessed, the use of drones has made it easier to do so today with the advancement in technology. For instance, a certain wildlife occurrence cannot be captured without the use of a drone. Look around you to find out places in which your drone photography will be required, places where people cannot easily access, and make your mark in that area.

Photographing Youth Activities

Since most parents love to have great pictures of their kids taken especially when growing up, either during school sporting event or in-house activities with family, you could look into how to earn some extra income through this. Select a convenient activity you can cover that does not affect your day job such as plays and boy scout or girl scout groups. Do not forget to get a license before photos of these kids to avoid being sued by parents or organizers or even both.

Write an eBook

The idea behind writing an eBook is to keep earning money off your articles rather than just selling them off to a website. This gives you the freedom to carry on with other activities with less stress. Choose a niche you think you have a better understanding of and write about it. It could be a photo-location guide or any other niche you can think of.

Write an Actual Book

These are hard copies of an eBook, and although they cost money to publish and print, you can still make some cash off it from good sales.

Sell Photography Equipment

Surprised, right? Don't be. Although you do not have to sell your personal camera, if you love selling things off on eBay purchases, selling some photography equipment at a good price can give you some extra cash.

The best part is that you will be able to do this on the side while keeping your full-time job.

Chapter 15: Side Hustles for Models

Aiming for a career as a model is both exciting and challenging all at the same time. Before you get started, you must be aware that you need an extra means of income to be able to settle your bills while you chase after your dreams of becoming a model. This is because it will take some time before you can build a reputation and get high-paying jobs. You are unlikely to earn huge paychecks at the early stage of your career. Therefore, you must be intelligent and find ingenious ways to fend for yourself while you still pursue your ambition of becoming a model. Payments for a job done sometimes takes up to 60 to 90 days or longer if you are not under a modeling agency that serves your best interest.

A model's schedule is very unpredictable as they are expected to work at weird hours and work at various locations. A model must be ready at all times when called upon. For you to be able to realize the dream of modeling, research has shown that it is paramount that a side job should be considered to generate sustainable income for the time being. Therefore, the ploy is getting a job that would not tamper with your aspiration.

Here are some side jobs to help you kick start your journey into the modeling industry:

Substitute Teacher

According to Aaron Marcus, a well-experienced coach and commercial model, one of the most desirable jobs for a model to be able to pull through their early stage in modeling is being a substitute teacher. The job of a substituted teacher allows you as a model to decide the time periods you desire to work, and it also pays well. So, if you can take as many teaching jobs as possible, you won't have difficulties settling your bills and pursuing your dreams at the same time. You should, however, be informed on the educational requirements to be eligible for the position of a substitute teacher, as they differ in every state. Some states will require a college diploma while other states won't. So, you are advised to go through the local school system where you want a job for more detailed information.

Fitness Instructor

As a model, it is only natural to always keep fit and be knowledgeable on how to maintain a perfect body, and, as such, you can consider the position of a fitness instructor. You can coach others through teaching Yoga, Zumba, running, or personal training. This is considered a great side job because it is very flexible, with considerably great pay. You have the advantage of meeting different amazing people and who knows, you might get a job as a fitness model.

Promotional Worker

In today's world, companies have graduated from solely engaging advertisement agencies to promote their products to outgoing, good-looking individuals to serve as brand ambassadors, event workers, and even as product demonstrators. This is a great job opportunity as you can always decide when to take or reject a job offer. You also get to work at a different location, such as an event cocktail or at a huge concert. You must, however, be aware of the kind of jobs you take, as some of these companies are not legitimate, you are advised to contact a professional company that will serve your best interest.

Temping

Have you ever considered working with a temp agency? This is a great side job opportunity if you are good with computers and a fast typist. Temp jobs are mostly considered stress-free office works that give you the needed opportunity to try out for auditions or bookings. If you are interested, look out for good temp agencies in the area you reside in. Some of these agencies specialize in modeling hubs or the entertainment industry.

Makeup Artist

Another side job to consider is finding work as a makeup artist within the modeling industry, especially if you are talented and passionate about it. Working as a makeup artist gives you the liberty to choose your working schedule. You can choose where you work and who you want to work with. A perk to this job is that you are within the modeling industry, where you will be able to gather valuable experiences and generate a good income enough for you to follow your ambition of modeling.

If you don't consider yourself a professional makeup artist but still have the desire to learn, various programs specialize in training makeup artists in perfecting their skills. Some of these organizations liaise with some makeup producing companies, which allow the students to use their products while training. Some of these organizations also offer certificates after the conclusion of the program. The good news is that these programs are flexible, giving you an ample amount of time to chase your dreams, and at the same time improve your creativity in the beauty line.

As a professional makeup artist, there are events and places where your skills as a makeup artist are needed and can serve you like a side job. They are:

- **Weddings**

A bride's dream is to look her very best on her wedding day. She is careful and selective on who does her makeup, and as a result, a quality makeup artist is needed. An ideal makeup artist is one who has understood and mastered the skills of using great and suitable products, also employing techniques to apply these products perfectly well on the bride's face. It is important that the overall application of the makeup complements the bride's skin tone. If a job is well done, the bride's squad will seek your services during their big day too or for any other events.

- **Photoshoot**

To get frequent gigs as a makeup artist, the perfect people to network with are professional photographers. They are always in contact with people from every sphere of life, from the fashion industry to the advertisement industry and everything in between. A photographer is known to always need a professional makeup artist to accomplish the photographer's creative look. Once you are in contact with five or six photographers, your cash flow will increase.

- **Holidays**

Halloweens are the perfect holiday season to show off your creative skills as a makeup artist, from creating a spooky look to creating a vampire look. Your excellence will get thousands or millions of likes on social media. That way, people will patronize you and offer you more jobs. Your skills are not limited to Halloween periods as haunted houses are also known to hire make-up artists to create ghost looks. This side job is flexible and allows you to showcase how creative you are.

- **Prom and Homecoming**

Prom and homecoming are known to be the biggest events in a high school year. Girls are likely to go all the way to look their best, and, as such, there will be an inexhaustible need for great professional makeup. This comes in very handy as a side job, since it happens once in a school year and it is a perfect way to generate an extra income, to pursue one's dream of becoming a model.

Chapter 16: Best Side Hustles for Speakers

Public speakers are known to have such oratory power and great tips on how one must get anything done. Their ability to speak well and motivate the crowd doesn't always translate to more income or the ability to make a good income from their career as a professional speaker.

The following are ways to earn a good income from side jobs in speaking:

Conference Presentations, Keynote Speakers, and Personal Platforms

When people think about professional speaking, they envision speakers who are paid for their expertise and ability to attract people to their events. So, to be able to make your career as speaker profitable through side jobs, you must position yourself strategically as an expert in what you do, so when people think about who is best for the job, they think of you.

If your niche is that of a personal-platform speaker, note that you are a brand. People will come from far and near to pay and hear you speak. You must make yourself known through all mediums possible so that the audience identifies with you when you are on stage. This way, you can also act as an influencer. Thus, you can sell companies products to your audience.

Be a Brand Ambassador

A speaker is known as one with a convincing power through his oratory skills. These skills are sought by companies and organizations who engage speakers as brand ambassadors, and in other cases, as an advocate. They will pay good money to have a speaker tell an audience about their products or organization in a captivating manner.

Be a Trainer

A professional speaker can act as a trainer through the impartation of knowledge to others. This training can be presented in the form of an institutional seminar, where the speaker takes his or her time to explain things in a subject in detail, taking you through the process of the subject matter. Unlike a keynote speaker, a trainer is not involved in the logistics of the event but solely has the primary duty of leading the seminar or workshop as the case may be. A keynote speaker, on the other hand, is known to present huge ideas that leave the audiences flabbergasted.

Packing Your Knowledge and Expertise

Creativity is an essential ingredient in developing more than one stream of income as a speaker. For instance, if you have an expatriate knowledge in web-development, it will be imprudent to share all you know at a single seminar or conference. It is best to create different themes in sharing your knowledge in web development, consequently providing platforms to make extra income.

Personal Services

Do not wait until you get a huge gig to speak before a large crowd to earn money. While waiting for the better gigs, you can engage in personal consultation services and coaching where you can share your knowledge one on one with a person or a small group. The advantage of doing this is that it gives you a break from your usual routine, giving you an opportunity to experience both worlds.

Chapter 17: Side Hustles for Musicians

It has become more glaringly apparent that making a living off music has become extremely difficult nowadays. The exceptions are very few especially in a world occupied with online music streaming and playlists. Many serious musicians have to worry more about making money off their vocation.

However, on the off chance that you want to make money being a musician while keeping your full-time income, there are a few side hustles that you can use in supplementing your income until you get your breakthrough.

Some of these side jobs for musicians include:

Cover Bands

Predominantly, this option is quite popular, but many musicians don't take the time to consider it due to the fear of being tagged unserious as well as not wanting to identify with another musician's music.

The benefits of the cover brand route cannot be over-emphasized. With an excellent style, musical experience, and viable location, you could earn thousands of dollars playing for clubs and events. Although it is expected that you get treated with the very thought of playing a cover band, the monetary benefit option it offers is one of a kind.

Music Therapist

Being a music therapist is one phenomenal choice for musicians looking forward to achieving excellence with their talent. From managing pain to special help education for traumatized people, the positive effects and benefits of music are just too immeasurable.

Nonetheless, not every musician possesses the right vibe to hit the right cord. It is more a groomed talent than merely ordinary. There are lots of exams to be taken, months of extensive training, as well as a certificate of issuance. Be that as it may, none of these can be compared to helping the musician pay off bills and giving back to society as well.

Music Critic/Blogger

Having adequate knowledge and a solid musical background is a catatonic credential for writing critiques and blog post for music. Over time, press outlets and blog owners have had pressing needs of wanting to hire competent music writers who are also passionate about what they do. You really cannot ask for more because the flexibility associated with the job type gives you the chance to do other pressing things without one affecting the other. As it is with every hustle, not every musician has the capacity to fit into the music writing gig efficiently.

Even if you turn out to be an excellent writer, there's no likelihood that you'd last in the venture especially if you are not so interested in it. And since the gig is one that would require you to stay updated musically and always listen to new music regularly, you really might not fancy that. But if you are to scale past these hurdles, you are on your way to earning a fortune from the music critique/writing profession.

Music Curator

Since many are tuning in to playlists, one job that musicians should vehemently accept wholeheartedly is a music curator position. Once you are knowledgeable enough about the different styles of music available and you have a great sense of good music, you are good to go. However, the position doesn't come without its challenges. Hence, there are some factors to consider.

Primarily, you need more than a passion for music to succeed in this venture. You need to display beyond doubts of being capable enough to handle in-depth music type knowledgeably as well as appreciating them.

Having done that, the next thing you'd need to possess is proven experience that suits different moods for different events.

Music Teacher and Mentor

Teaching music is quite a common niche for musicians. However, there are reasons why it is popular.

The thing is, the society we live in today holds music teachers in high regard, and as such people would pay a lot to learn good music. The teacher also would have predominant control over their schedule and number of students to take lessons on for. The time and venue is also duly your call, and you make virtually all the decisions.

However, teaching music is not something everyone can do. Some musicians, during their learning days, have been tutored by bad teachers and ended up hating the experience. Teaching is one act that requires patience, tolerance, and perseverance, especially when dealing with kids. However, you cannot compare the experience you had while learning an instrument to real life patience while teaching. If you've got the time, energy, and tolerance, teaching is one big act that can safely put food on your table and offer you a lifelong income for the time been.

If, by any chance, you are the type that loves traveling and love learning more to expand your knowledge, you'd come across great websites and online platforms that are really great for helping you teach instruments with ease as much as possible as well as giving you a broader range of being able to go into music production, composition, orchestration, as well as musical mentorship.

Sound Tech

On the off chance that you have vast experience in different musical gigs, you'd likely know something tangible to supplement your musical experience, and live sound is probably one of them. Once you are able to improve this skill, and you have succeeded in crafting out a potential for yourself for securing a better job in the future.

Try out more with your local connections, and see if the music venues around need some work done behind their soundboard. If you prefer touring, trying sourcing out for sound tech bands that suit your style and hit the road with them.

Cruise Ship Performer

Tentatively, cruise performances tend to be rigid, but if you're homely enough to endure until the end, you'd have succeeded in making out a gig for yourself that would, in the long run, pay off the bills for you as well as help you hone your musical skills.

Wedding DJ

Are you able to play a broad range of music that effectively matches the mood of a crowd in any event? Why not try expanding these skills at a game close to you, especially a wedding and fill up as a DJ. This way, you'd be gaining more ground around your axis and shunning off competition as much as you can.

Music Store Salesperson

Somehow, it sounds a little weird to work in a record or music store, but the truth is, it's enjoyable being around instruments, records, and musical gear all day. Although you might not earn a big paycheck at the end of the day, you stand the chance of helping others make the right choices in their selection of music all the way.

Music Venue Bartender

Though bartending isn't related to music directly, it's a great way to maintain an excellent musical pulse especially when it is a cool venue. The tips you'd get are just an add-on for building a formidable network opportunity with other music geeks that come around.

Piano Tuner

You don't have to be a pianist to be a tuner. Once you can listen deeply and understand the instrument, you stand the chance of getting hired as a tuner. At some point, you may need some bits of training to hone your skills and keep readily in demand extensively. Once done, you'd be flexible enough to work just anywhere either as a pianist or piano fixer.

Chapter 18: Side Hustle for Gamers

A great deal of expertise and marketability has a lot of influence in the world of live-stream gaming. Playing video games has become such a big-time profession amongst people nowadays that it is gradually getting there in terms of parity with main physical sports.

Gamers are now building their creative skills as institutions of higher learning have scholarships for e-gamers. Many websites are out there that now even teach you as a gamer the means of making cool money off playing games via live streaming.

The world of gaming is in a straight comparison to that of the regular, routine working world. It is typically thought by many people to be linked to people who are introverts or adults who have no better use of their leisure time.

However, the two contrasting worlds are slowly but surely beginning to form a merger, with ardent gamers now making a good career out of video gaming and workplaces having video games through which their staff can playfully unwind during the lunch-break hour.

You can earn money off video games. However, this is also not a sure means of becoming extremely wealthy. You would not be able to resign from your day job though you would make a few extra bucks here and there while in the gaming world, even if it is for just a few hours in the evening.

Listed below are some of the ways in which you can make money as an ardent gamer. Surely not all of them are failsafes, but most are legal and sure ways of generating income. You can also carry out your own research on other ways apart from those listed, and make extra inroads into your financial gains.

Earn Money Via Livestream Gaming

A lot of games nowadays stream live, have players lining up against each other live, and have monetary rewards for players. This is a way through which video game freaks make money to sustain themselves. You can make financial income playing games by:

Become the Gaming Champion

Some video game firms have tournaments online that reward the overall winner financially. Video gaming site Litcoin provides a live-streaming platform for gamers online to compete against each other on their games like *Brothers in Arms*, *Squad Duty*, and *Legends of Tomorrow*. Your reward for passing stages, which you can use as payment for buying real-world goods could be Bitcoin.

Some major gaming firms provide all of their gamers with free entry to competitions hosted by it. The overall winner takes home a cash price as a reward. Almost all the popular blockbuster games have leagues or tournament that gamers compete in for monetary rewards.

Selective Gameplay on Websites

Many commercially-viable websites give monetary rewards to visitors of their sites when they play games via their web links. You would receive many offers when you become a member. All you have to do is sign up or register with them, browse through their gaming offers, pick a game to play and start earning whilst you play.

Games Account Trading

The advent of gaming online has made opening an online gaming account mandatory. In your account, you have a number of achievements to attain via game currencies, consumables, equipment, and so on. The more time you put into achieving points, the extra money you have deposited into your gaming account which, in turn, raises the value of your gaming account.

Many gamers are too bothered to put in the extra hard work and hours to build a good gaming level but rather just buy a gaming account they feel attracted to. A niche has thereby developed where gaming accounts are sold and bought for a certain fee. If you find a good gaming account to buy, put up an advert, and you will get a lot of gamers willing to sell their accounts.

Many gaming regulations for online gaming exist. eBay, for example, does not allow for virtual property sales on its platform, because of cases of fraud. They also have websites where virtual properties selling takes place as smoothly as possible.

When you want to buy stuff in the game, try to verify whether it is legal to do before buying in accordance with the game terms and conditions.

Selling Virtual Properties

There is also selling properties virtually in the gaming world. *Second Life* video gamers can build landed properties virtually over time and either lease it out to fellow gamers or outright sell it at a decent price. There is evidence that there is real money, and lots of people have made profit by selling their virtual property through Livestream gaming.

You have games where improving on what exists in the game could earn you money as you become famous through fellow gamers visiting your gameplay live stream. You could market it as well, and before you know it, your fellow gamers would start a bidding process, with you giving it out to the highest bidder for very good financial returns.

The *Brothers in Arms* trilogy is a very good example where buying and selling of virtual property take place for money.

Games Boosting and Coaching Lessons

If you are an expert in a number of games, and people seek your advice on how to attain a certain level in those games, you could become a good coach online to fellow gamers. Enough gamers would pay you for such expertise especially if you happen to be a proficient coach.

For you to have attained a certain high level of expertise, you surely would have competed with other top gamers in the gaming world. You can advertise yourself on Google or a few social media platforms.

Boosting is another thing that is entirely different from coaching. In boosting, experts in the game can help a fellow average gamer in games involving different gamers to reach certain levels and achievements in the game. This helps to increase their ranking in the overall leaderboard.

Game boosting has become an illegal act in a lot of online games, which means gamers are desperately paying top dollar to acquire the services of a gamer with the expertise to help them.

Create a YouTube Gaming Channel

This means of getting money as a gamer is time consuming and takes a lot of dedication and commitment. What makes it more daunting is the fact that in comparison with other means for getting money as a gamer listed here, this is the means with an overall high rate of failure. But, if it is done right, you could end up making substantial financial gains.

You can utilize your YouTube fan base by first recording your gameplay as you are playing, edit it, and add your voice as you narrate it to make the video captivating and entertaining. Upload your video to your channel and wait for people or fellow gamers to view it and possibly give it a thumbs-up. Your number of views gives you money.

The most visited YouTube channel in the world is owned by a 24-year-old Swede by the name of Kjellberg Felix, who generates tons of money year by year through ads that run on his YouTube videos alone. His videos are just made up of gameplay times, with a little acting and humor to spice it up. He is now a multi-millionaire only from the money he makes from his YouTube videos.

Be a Game Tester

Some gaming firms would, first of all, give out their new games undergoing development to gamers they know are video game freaks. They become the firm's outside game testers. Of course, you get paid for being part of the testing gig, but it is not as lucrative in comparison to other ways of making money as a gamer mentioned above.

Chapter 19: Side Hustle for Animal Lovers

Do you love animals? Then why not make a fortune off of it? Even if you don't in all sincerity have passion for animals, you still can make it a side hustle for making extra bucks for a living.

On a quick note, it is imperative to know that every personal interest can be monetized even from making it a side hustle. So long as a passion remains viable, it can be monetized. All you need to do is to get the right notions and guidelines toward monetizing it.

Below are some side hustles to try out as an animal lover:

Animal-Related Content Writing

Do you possess the technical and writing ability to churn out optimized contents for blogs?

Overly, the amount you'd be making depends predominantly on your content writing quality and budgets of people you'd be working for or with. Typically, the average pay per word is between 10-50 cents. Also, you need to understand that time is of the essence in determining how well you get more jobs as the more deliverables you can deliver within stipulated time, the more confidently your client would outsource more jobs to you.

Pet Photography

If your camera type is high-quality and can produce excellent images, it would be entirely more comfortable for you to begin making money from pet photographs. Here, you don't have to have an HD camera (although it's a plus if you do) before you can start taking pictures because your smartphone camera might be enough to give you the professional polish needed.

So, what to do? Get some picture samples of pets and animals to develop your portfolio in which you can post on any pet-dedicated platforms and websites. Averagely, you'd make between the range of $150 to $180 from pet photography. However, the price might reduce if you prefer taking pictures in a natural setting than a studio. Nonetheless, you'd still be able to make a decent amount weekly. So, pick yourself and develop your portfolio from your or a friend's or family pets or animals.

You see that a lot of opportunities abound for entrepreneurs that have a liking for animals. It is one heck of a side hustle to practice your passion, make extra bucks, and still maintain your original job.

Cleaning up After Dogs

For most pet owners, picking up poop is one job that they detest doing, but it is inevitable because a failure to do so could result in diseases for the animals involved.

So, since it is a must-do job that a pet owner doesn't like to do, why not take the responsibility and relieve the pet owner from the stress for pay? That is if you can stomach it. You could likely serve as the neighborhood cleaner and also as the health inspector for the mammals. You'd earn good money from it to take care of your bills too.

Your charges, however, would be based on the size of the yard and number of pets you're taking care of. For recurring clients, you can decide to offer them a discount to balance fairness on both sides.

However, you should know that your service wouldn't just advertise itself. Hence, you'd need to let people know the services you offer. Joining a reputable company that offers such service is another added advantage for getting such jobs from your neighborhood and beyond.

Dog Training

If you can train dogs well to respect and understand their owner's wish, then it would be best if you take it up as a side hustle vocation.

Many pet owners love when their pets obey them, but they rarely have the time to engage their pets into such training. As a trainer, you can tell them the basic 'How-to(s)' to allow them to get along with their dogs with ease.

Certification after training is essential, so it would be beneficial if you sign up with a certificate-issuing institute to get enough training before training a dog.

Pet Blogging

Pet blogging is another well-paid gig that could fetch you bucks in case you choose an attractive and highly-sought out topic.

For some people who are passionate about keeping pets and animals generally, there's a high likelihood of you having a thing or two to write about these furry creatures. If affirmative, why not consider starting up a blog to voice out what you have to say and what interests you about such pets.

Focusing on the general topic about pets is extensively broad, so it would be better if you focus your niche on some pets. This way you'd be able to provide well-optimized contents which you can monetize, advertise affiliate products, and promote ads in the long run.

Pets Products Manufacture

Creating pet products can be as rewarding as other mentioned gigs in this piece.

So, if you are the type that can create products such as baked treats for animals, toys, or clothes, then you can make good money from selling them to owners of pet shops or individual owners as well. There are also some online platforms that give you the chance to market your products to all and sundry.

For this gig, you might need some capital to start up before scaling up. You could partner with pet business owners to create an audience for those who'd patronize you.

Pet Sitting

You might be among the type that loves pets but doesn't enjoy doing so at the comfort of other's homes. So, why not consider converting your home for fixing pets on a scheduled basis?

Some pet owners would rather leave their pets in the warm, loving comfort of a home than any other place, so yours might be the next call.

Groom Pets

Pets grooming require skills and training to actualize. So, if you have what it takes to do it, then you are in for making real cash from it by making it a side hustle.

You need to know that there is more to taking care of a pet than just cleaning it. So, you must make sure you are patient enough to use your energy in excelling as a professional in the business.

Additionally, you need to have comprehensive knowledge about animal behavior to know what is wrong with the pet you're handling, from when it is hungry to when it is sick.

Typically, the United States doesn't require that you are certified before you can groom a dog. However, it is usually of an advantage to have the certificate to do so.

Walk Pets

Primarily, pets need to exercise themselves, but due to the busy routine of their owners, sometimes they don't stand a chance to do so. So, if you step up to fill in then this might be the enjoyable gig that you could use to augment your income.

Chapter 20: Side Hustles for Accountants

There are a lot of people who are quite gifted with numbers, finding it very easy to work with math in their heads without having to make use of a pen and paper. Most of these people end up as accountants or financial analysts, but accountants are the focus of this section.

The average salary an accountant gets paid is around $67,190 according to a salary statistic carried out by salary.com. This is quite a substantial amount of money to earn as a salary for most content, but for extravagant accountants, who could have debts of over a $100,000, this is not nearly enough. Below are ways you can make extra money as an accountant.

They include:

Bookkeeping Services

Bookkeeping is the number one side hustle an accountant can engage in. The job of a bookkeeper does vary depending on the nature of the business. A bookkeeper performs the role of documenting the various transactions carried out by a company on a day-to-day basis. Therefore, a bookkeeper should be an individual that is very organized and be quite knowledgeable about many bookkeeping procedures.

You can perform many bookkeeping services for clients in your spare time as long as you are very organized and deliver your finished work on time. You can seek out some bookkeeping vacancies via sites like Craigslist.

Taxation Services

Many things could go incredibly wrong when one wants to fill and file in his or her tax returns personally. You could fall foul of the tax laws if you forget to fill in a particular item or wrongfully fill in places you are not supposed to in tax forms.

Many people find it quite a burden to take time out to prepare their tax sheets, thereby running late in submitting their tax returns to the relevant tax authorities. You, as an accountant, have the responsibility of making sure they file their tax returns when due. The best time to engage in this hustle? The first quarter of every year is a great time to participate in this side business and make quite a financial gain. This is because a lot of people who have to file in their tax returns before the deadline of each fiscal year desperately seek the services of accountants. You can get a lot of clients who want their tax sheets prepared and filed with the tax authorities if you start advertising your services as early as January of a new year.

Creating How-To Guides

When it comes to the knowledge of how numbers work, most people, in general, do not know even a quarter as much as an accountant does. This knowledge can be turned into monetary value by an accountant through the creation of "how-to" guides. An excellent example of this is the issue of taxes. A lot of people find problems of taxation an annoying and daunting task but still want to a know how the tax system works. You could create a simple how-to guide as it relates to issues of general taxation, the filing in of tax returns, and make some money off the sales of your guide. You could also create how-to guides on other financial matters, and this is made all the more comfortable with the modern technology available nowadays. The creation of a how-to guide should not take that much time.

Consultancy Services

Since accountants are experts in their chosen area of specialization, they could offer their services as consultants. This side hustle covers quite an array of accounting services that you could provide to clients, which could include bookkeeping and taxation as has been discussed earlier in this article. You could also help out the client with some essential accounting work, and all depends on exactly what the client wants from you.

Auditory Services

Auditing is the last side business an accountant could do to make extra cash. Many clients are on the lookout for accountants to help them carry out auditing of their small and big companies like supermarkets, manufacturing industries, and shops, just to mention a few. Auditing is mainly carried out to check for cases of fraudulent practices by any member of staff in a firm. It also helps in the confirmation of receivables into the account of an establishment and accounts they have with a third party.

As an accountant, you can try your hands on any of the above-listed ways as a means of making that extra financial income.

Chapter 21: Side Hustles you can start for $10,000 to $50,000

The constant change in technology has created a wide range of opportunity for startups such as bioplastic packaging, meal kits, and whatever else you can think of. A lot of businesses and opportunities have been created as a result of meeting the demands of consumers.

There are certain things one must look out for before investing in any business. These include finding out the demand rate for the product or service, competition, and pricing of product and services.

This will allow you to evaluate how profitable the business is. It is also advisable to use reliable potential customers of yours as a mentor that will guide you in creating the right business plan.

Below are a few business ideas you can begin for $10,000 to $50,000.

3D Printing

3D printing involves taking an engineering drawing of either CAD or CAM and printing it out. Over the years a greater number of 3D companies have been established, but there are still two profitable opportunities in 3D printing:

Producing spare parts of equipment that are no longer produced like the pinball machines.

Providing manufacturers with low-volume parts of equipment. You will make more profit if you produce CAD/CAM drawings.

Food Kit Manufacturing

You can start up a profitable business by merely producing food kits such as spices for veggies, starches, meat, and baking ingredients for desserts. Although there are a few established small businesses in this field, there is still room for more start-ups. The challenge, however, is the lack of FDA-approved manufacturers. One way to begin is to produce kits for sellers at the farmer's markets or craft fairs.

Custom Assembly

Manufacturing of custom computers has been an existing business for years now. Traditional manufacturing cannot produce one to five units. Therefore, they area potential for custom assembly startup businesses that sell 10 to 100 units as well are potential customers of custom construction until they are capable of building larger volumes of products.

Electronic wire assembly and welding are a few areas where custom manufacture could specialize in. This is because businesses that lack the necessary equipment to carry out such activities would outsource for them.

Organic Herbal Cosmetic Creams

Organic cosmetics are gradually gaining grounds in the market today, and there are currently lots of organic or herbal cosmetic creams being sold at the farmer's market, specialty stores, and craft fairs. These are products manufactured with natural plant-based ingredients other than chemicals. Many people are venturing into this line of business and creating their own unique formulas.

It is best for companies that desire to partner with these manufacturers to ensure their products are produced in an FDA-approved facility. This can become a profitable business as entrepreneurs lacking in manufacturing capacity outsource it, and the products gain acceptance.

Heavy Duty Canvas Sewing

These are manufactures that specialize in the outdoor industry such as RVs, camping, boats, and other related products. The good thing about this kind of manufacturing is the fact that there is an increase in outdoor activities and lots of companies organize at least three shows yearly for consumers to attend.

You can attract more customers through the kind of relationship you have with retailers. A retailer that likes you will provide you customers in need of a custom canvas services.

Bioplastic Packaging

Low waste packaging today now includes items such as sandwich containers, potato chips bags, coffee cups, and take-away packs. Every bioplastic producer has the option to either buy or manufacture what they use. This bioplastic packaging is mostly used in food stores, restaurants, and coffee houses.

Small Hole Machining

The advancement in technology has led to the manufacture of small-sized electronics or equipment that 3D printers cannot handle. There are two ways of creating small holes in small-sized machines: laser and micromachining. The demand for various kinds of small machines keeps rising, and small entrepreneurs can take advantage of these opportunities, and create a business of it for themselves.

Metal Casting

This involves recycling used metals to something more useful and selling them. It also includes making use of sand molds to produce metal parts. Businesses with low volume productions or those into prototyping and creation of repair parts that are out of production can utilize this. A cheap furnace might not be able to do justice to high-quality steel but can work correctly for mild steel, bronze, aluminum, cast iron, and lead.

Vacuum or Thermoform Molding

Vacuum or thermoform molding is a suitable type of business for startups because the requirements are readily available. Vacuum forming involves the heating up of a plastic material to a specific temperature, then stretching it onto a mold, and a vacuuming the heated plastic against the mold. A startup with less financial capacity can make use of wood as the mold while the aluminum mold is best for more massive production.

Many manufacturers with a significant requirement of 250 to 500 units make use of vacuum formed parts when it is not feasible to get the injection molding equipment. The ATM housings and sign industry are the major customers of thermoforming manufacturers.

Wood Promotional Products

Although the regular wood shop is a good source of income, promotional products such as plaques offer more to the manufacturers even though they produce the same product. Most wooden promotional products are more valuable than regular promo products. This is a good line of business that a startup entrepreneur could look into. You can attract more buyers through building your own website, having a promotional product magazine, and supplying to sellers.

Chapter 22: Side Hustles to Begin Under $10,000

For any great idea to become a successful reality, it needs to be fed with passion, dedication, and commitment for it to thrive. Not all businesses require huge start-up capital investments.

In setting up a side hustle, you need to know what it takes to set up the business, carry out feasibility studies, know the skills you might have to acquire to successfully start the business, and the labor market rates as it pertains to the billing of clients.

You also have to know what type of business you intend to run, such as either a small-scale business or a full-time or part-time business that dictates how many staff-hours you need to invest in making it a viable, reliable company. This, in turn, gives you an idea of the type of potential clients you would be offering your services to.

You can seek out professional guidelines in setting up a business, financial tips to maintaining a business, and business writings on websites that have helpful tips about the business setup.

You might have lots of business ideas but be afraid to venture into them because of the monetary investment it would require setting them up successfully.

Here, we will be taking a look at the side hustles you can easily start without huge monetary investment.

They include:

Image Consultancy Services

The image consulting sector is as lucrative as it is exciting. You gain a lot financially from bringing out the best in people and making them believe in themselves. You can help someone going for an interview to pass the interviewing process successfully, help to build the self-esteem or worth of people, and also help people do great with first impressions.

This can be attained through some ways such as:

- Training on social etiquette
- Training on handshaking and body posture
- Perusing through the present personae and working on a new one
- Consulting services for wardrobes
- Development of skills to communicate much more better

Your potential clients could be the politically elite, top corporate business executives, media celebrities, marketing professionals, public motivational speakers, singles who are looking to be hitched up, people searching for jobs in the labor market, and patients who are undergoing rehabilitative therapy.

Home Care Services

The non-medical home care sector is expanding as the population of the aged in the United States is constantly increasing. The services proffered in this expanding industry are:

- Medication reminders

- Preparing meals
- Offering companionship
- Housekeeping services
- Running errands
- Getting groceries
- Laundry services

Patients in need of rehabilitative services after suffering from particular injuries, pregnant women, and people who live with disabilities are among the people who would seek out your services. It is an easy business to venture into as it does not require one to be vastly experienced but just someone who is reliable and compassionate. The requirements to start this business as an individual or to set up an establishment is to have insurance.

Makeup Artist

This business has a lot of potential as you could be of service to TV stations, doing the makeup for their presenters or a makeup artist to the bride on her engagement and wedding day. You will also be needed in the entertainment and filming industry, where you do makeup for the celebrities in that sector.

You could decide to be a makeup artist on the go or have an office for makeup and manicures and pedicures, or offer your services to an already established company.

You can further your clientele base by attending various events around your neighborhood, making contacts with some wedding and event planners and other stakeholders.

Become a Physical Health Trainer

Certification is mandatory before you can begin this business, which can be recieved after attending classes at certified aerobics school which you can learn about from the necessary regulatory bodies on physical fitness in America. You can then start the business by serving people at their homes, places of work, or find a place to open up a fitness and wellness center, where you provide fitness training services to either a group or for individuals. People with disabilities, citizens in the senior cadre, pregnant women, and top business executives that are extremely busy but desire to be fit are your potential customers.

Upholstery Services

You could be a carpenter or just have a flair or skills about carpentry and wooding work, and you can start a mobile carpentry service. If your services are top quality, your clients will be made up of house movers, managers of properties, personal business entrepreneurs, as well as the top and middle rated class hoteliers and diners.

Decorating Services

If you are highly talented with decoration, this is a good business to delve into. This business need to have someone with highly creative skills in designing in order to be successful. You check out the bodies invested with a regulation of Interior Designers to know what you need to start the business. For your marketing strategy, you can make use of the interactive media that you have accounts with to advertise your decorating services, showing locations where you have decorated with pictures that showcase your decorative skills.

Handyperson

In the beginning this business, you need to have a flair or acquire the necessary skills required of jobs such as carpentry, plumbing, masonry, or wiring. You also need to be the kind of person that knows something about everything. When you give out quality services in these type of basic jobs, referrals will help you get repeated client calls and even new clients along the way as your usual clients will help spread the word of your competence. You could check out the Associations inclined with this business regulation on how to get started.

Commercialized Cleaning Up

You could start by offering your cleaning services on a much larger scale in comparison to small-scale residential cleaners. Commercial cleaning on its own generates a lot of money, running into billions of dollars. It also involves washing high-rise building windows, emptying dustbins, and refilling inventories of firms with basic toiletries. To start this business, you can look up different brochure of regulatory bodies.

Waste Disposal

With the aid of a few dustbins, waste disposal bags, and a truck for easy carriage of waste, you can become a neighborhood waste removal man. You can bill your clients by looking at truckloads weight, quotations that are industry inclined, or on an hourly-based charge to help them in disposing of their house waste.

Chimney Sweeper

If you have experience with masonry repairs, you can become a chimney sweeper or rebuilder. You can repaint chimneys with success as well as do sealing up of chimneys. You just have to buy the necessary equipment associated with this kind of job and undergo training necessary to carry out the job successfully.

Cleaning Window Covers

In the countries that make up the continent North America, windows blinds are a very popular item both at home or in offices. You can become a window blinds cleaner with the aid of ultrasonic equipment that can clean window blinds efficiently without making necessary working parts of the blinds to malfunction.

Car Dents Removal Service

You can start up this type of business since not all dents on cars require a cover-up using car paint. All you need is to purchase the necessary equipment that is used explicitly for removing the little dents. You could add other car-related services like tinting of car windows, repairing window chips, and detailing automobiles.

Bicycle Repairing Service

For a mechanically-inclined individual or a person who has a flair for repairing all kinds of items, becoming a bicycle repairer does not require huge capital to startup. All that is needed is a garage or another space that is big enough to grow your workshop for repairing faulty bicycles. You can market your services in the neighborhood where your business is located utilizing radio advertisements and fliers.

Become an Event/Party Planner

Many people desire to hold occasions such as anniversary parties, luncheons, or graduation parties but cannot cope with the hassles involved with such. You can quickly step in to solve these problems by making yourself good event/party planner. You can help your clients to prepare invitation cards, help with locating an excellent venue for the event, and source out competent MCs, caterers, and photographers, all in a bid to make the event a success.

Become a Wedding Planner

A wedding planner takes up all the responsibilities associated with the successful planning of a wedding ceremony. This makes the wedding couple worry less and feel a smaller amount of pressure on their wedding day, all at the expense of an affordable budget. You could start up this business without much capital. You can Google up a few helpful tips on how to successfully begin your wedding-planner business.

House Rental Services

This is a job that is easy and has good potential for earnings. The financial lucrativeness of this business manifests during the holidays. All it takes is a little money to acquire an old bounce house at a cheaper rate as opposed to wanting to get one that is brand new on the market.

Start a Childcare Center

With the rising cost of living nowadays, both parents have to take up jobs in order to cope with meeting their family needs. This could take a toll on the welfare of their kids. You can be a solution provider here by setting up a child daycare or an after-school center. The startup capital to venture into it is not huge. By the time you have quite a good setup, you might find yourself declining numerous parent requests because of the workload.

Chapter 23: Conclusion

There is no shortage of side hustle ideas that you can take advantage of. Take the first step to action, and get things moving right away. Although this is a very long list of side hustle ideas, you need to understand that there are a lot of different ways to earn cash on the side, and this list is only a starting point.

Nonetheless, this list is genuine. What it implies is that it is easy to fail with any of these ideas, but you will certainly be able to use any of them to get the financial freedom that you desire. Like any jobs, side hustles are not stress-free and they require you to put in some extra effort.

Each of these ideas require you to hustle harder than your counterparts, work smarter, take a moment to teach yourself, and execute it properly. Simply said, this is not a get-rich-fast scheme. These ideas will need your passion and sweat, and because lots of individuals won't include that needed dedication, winning can come much more comfortably if you work for it.

Don't forget that with the appropriate effort, passion, and ideas, nothing beats your own business providing you the life you desire and the income you deserve. We live in an amazing time where with the appropriate attitude and approach, you can begin your business machine for generating cash.

Don't forget to go into your side hustle with your eyes open. Set up your expectations and goals. Also, know when to quit. If one side hustle is not making progress, leave it, and try another one. Change is essential, and nothing lasts forever.

Now, get out there and start side hustling!

www.ingramcontent.com/pod-product-compliance
Lightning Source LLC
Chambersburg PA
CBHW021814170526
45157CB00007B/2588